PETE DOHERTY

My Prodigal Son

D0492512

The author and publisher wish to thank the following for use of copyright material:

Peter Doherty for the poem 'Smoking', p. 51, and 'The Bow Poem', p. 82

AmyJo Doherty for the poem 'Everyone Wants a Story', p. 155

Discovery House Publishers for lines from *Our Daily Bread*

The Literary Trustee of the late Patience Strong for 'Tell Them', p. 192. No reproduction permitted without authorisation. All rights controlled

PETE DOHERTY

My Prodigal Son

JACQUELINE DOHERTY

headline

First published in 2006
by HEADLINE PUBLISHING GROUP

1

Hardback: 10-digit ISBN 0 7553 1608 8
13-digit ISBN 978 0 7553 1608 3
Trade paperback: 10-digit ISBN 0 7553 1631 2
13-digit ISBN 978 0 7553 1631 1

Cataloguing in Publication Data is available from the British Library

Typeset in Perpetua by Avon DataSet Ltd, Bidford on Avon, Warwickshire

Printed and bound in Great Britain by Clays Ltd, St Ives plc

Headline's policy is to use papers that are natural, renewable and
recyclable products and made from wood grown in sustainable forests. The
logging and manufacturing processes are expected to conform to the
environmental regulations of the country of origin.

HEADLINE PUBLISHING GROUP
A division of Hodder Headline
338 Euston Road
London NW1 3BH

Every effort has been made to fulfil requirements with regard to reproducing
copyright material. The author and publisher will be glad to rectify any
omissions at the earliest opportunity.

www.headline.co.uk
www.hodderheadline.com

Oh! there is an enduring tenderness in the love of a mother to her son that transcends all other affections of the heart. It is neither to be chilled by selfishness, nor daunted by danger, nor weakened by worthlessness, nor stifled by ingratitude. She will sacrifice every comfort to his convenience; she will surrender every pleasure to his enjoyment; she will glory in his fame, and exult in his prosperity: — and, if misfortune overtake him, he will be the dearer to her from misfortune; and if disgrace settle upon his name, she will still love and cherish him in spite of his disgrace; and if all the world beside cast him off, she will be all the world to him.

Washington Irving

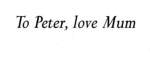

To Peter, love Mum

Contents

Acknowledgements		ix
Author's Note		xiii
1	The Prodigal Son	1
2	Fear Knocks at the Door	19
3	A Baby . . . and a Shambles	37
4	The Pen is Mightier than the Sword	53
5	Time to Move	69
6	The Big Issue	85
7	For Pete's Sake	97
8	Rumours Fly	123
9	What a Waste!	141
10	Everyone Wants a Story	155
11	Keeping the Faith	175
12	Nothing is Wasted	201
13	Waking to a Nightmare	219
	Postscript	233
	Afterword: A Note From Peter Doherty Senior	235

Acknowledgements

W ITH A THANKFUL heart I show my gratitude to all who have helped me tell my story:

To those who believed in it from day one.

To those who have prayed for 'the Peter Problem', please continue.

To those people, and there are many, who have tried so hard to help.

To my work colleagues, who have kept me buoyant and never asked questions.

To my grandson, Astile, who put a smile back on his grandad's face.

To Simon Benham, who made it all possible.

To Alex Hannaford, who held my trust and never betrayed me, and who helped me write this book. Alex came into my life one morning in the late summer of 2005. It had been a hectic morning; the telephone had not stopped ringing with calls from journalist after journalist. I was sitting by the phone, crying, when it rang again: 'I'm writing a book called *Last of the Rock Romantics* – it's about your son,' Alex told me. I burst into sobs, whilst a very apologetic young man set about trying to restore the damage he thought he'd caused. I explained that I didn't really mind what was printed about Peter, provided it was the truth. He was very kind and I told him that I, too, was writing a book. He didn't try to persuade me to talk to him but asked if he might send me his *curriculum vitae*, which he did in due course. It was a heartening and credible CV and, quite apart from all the work he had accomplished in his life, the one thing that stood out and touched my heart was that he was a volunteer crew member for the Thames Lifeboat. The word 'volunteer' means such a lot to me. We kept in touch over the months. He never imposed. He never assumed.

We were not to meet until 12 March 2006, Peter's twenty-seventh birthday. As I had grown to trust Alex over the months, I called him the previous day and said that I was ready to show him a few sample chapters of my book. We sat in Waterloo Station for an hour and he offered me his support and trust. As we parted company, me on my way to Peter's for the obligatory birthday jig, he on his way to find me an agent, he probably never saw the tears in my eyes as I mumbled under my breath: 'His mother must be very proud.'

I'm well known for my love of Latin phrases, so this one is for Alex. *Multi faman, coscientum pauci verenteur.* Many fear their reputation, few their conscience.

— Acknowledgements —

But this book is mostly for other mothers who have shared their story with me.

Dominus Tecum

Author's Note

The unlikely story . . . of a likely lad
Peter the drug addict
Peter the prisoner
Peter the errant father
Peter the poet
Peter the prolific writer
Peter the singer
Peter my son, my prodigal son.

How does one begin to express or define another human being? Even when that other human being has been borne of one's own blood, borne of one's own flesh? Even writing about one's self is such a difficult task, and can depend upon so many factors: one's mood, one's perception of life, and the desire to bare one's soul with a given audience. Removing the façade that has been so carefully built to portray to the world what you want them to perceive is a formidable task.

So this is *my* story. My story has no ending as yet. With the best will in the world, I have attempted to recount my story as the mother of Peter Doherty Junior. This is the truth as I see it.

When we require peace we must prepare for war, and I know there will be more tears and unending prayers to come.

During the last three years, I have witnessed the media interest in my son turn into media frenzy. This book is about how I have coped and how I am still coping – and, if it should help just one other person, then my efforts will not have been in vain.

Chapter 1

The Prodigal Son

Nosce telpsum – Know thyself

MY SON IS Peter Doherty. You may know him as Pete. You may know him as Britain's most notorious drug addict. You may not have heard of him. He was in a band called The Libertines and is currently in a band called Babyshambles.

History is strewn with stories of fallen pop idols, fragile film stars and troubled talents of all kinds. Someone once told me a story about a famous singer-songwriter in the Seventies who was carried onto the stage, placed on a stool and, after a superb performance, carried off again. I remember laughing about it at the time, never giving a thought to his poor mother and how she must be feeling. Never in my wildest nightmares imagining that someone, someday, would be doing the same thing to my son.

Let me begin this story with when the 'Peter Problem' began.

It was December 2002 and we were to spend a family Christmas in Germany, where my husband Peter and I were living at the time. Peter and his elder sister AmyJo had come over from London, where they both lived, although in different areas. Emily, their younger sister, had already broken up from her boarding school in the south of England for the holidays. Peter senior, who is in the Army, was, at the time, Second-in-Command of a Signals Regiment based near a border town called Elmpt. From there it was just a short journey to the beautiful city of Roermond in Holland. We lived twenty minutes away from the Army Camp in a very pretty German town called Wildenrath. The nearest city was Moenchengladbach.

Even then, AmyJo had arrived alone as Peter had missed his flight home. But he had phoned to say he would be arriving the following day. This caused me little concern because we knew his life was very busy and were grateful that he was just coming home at all.

Peter was to be with us for five days. I clearly remember thanking him for making time in his busy schedule to come home and *sleep* with us! The band he was in, The Libertines, had just recently been enjoying a small success. They were overjoyed to have been signed to the Rough Trade record label.

Normally we'd spend the entire five days out and about, joking around, having fun, but when Peter arrived home this time he was exhausted and hadn't slept for several days – I didn't know why. I put it down to burning the candle at both ends and wasn't overly worried, just glad to have the family together. Of his five days at home, he probably slept for four of them, just waking long enough to eat and visit the bathroom.

The only other unusual behaviour was that he was uncharacteristically belligerent. Normally, over the Christmas period, it would be open house at many of the military families' homes and my children knew a lot of the children on the camp. I remember that the son of a family friend came in and the ever-friendly, ever-sociable Peter was quite rude — so I pulled him up on it. He'd usually tell a joke, go out of his way to be friendly, to make any guest in our home feel more than welcome; but, today, his body language showed disinterest. You would have thought he'd have been happier than ever, but he wasn't interested in conversation and this was completely out of character. I put it down to tiredness.

The next serious alarm bell was that he came to the Christmas dinner table wearing a vest and jeans. His hair was long and messy and his skin was pale. I have a photograph of him pulling a Christmas cracker with a snarl on his face, taken actually as a joke — but there it was. He usually liked to dress up for the family Christmas dinner, making a grand entrance. Not for him a t-shirt. He would normally enter the room wearing a cravat, a waistcoat and trousers and crisp white shirt with an air of Oscar Wilde about him. I did actually ask him to go and get dressed and he complied. His tiredness, his rudeness, his appearance were small things in themselves, but the pointers were there . . . and I missed them. All of them.

It had begun. The Peter Problem.

Since Peter had first left home in September 1997, to study English at Queen Mary and Westfield University in East London, whenever I caught sight of him with his sleeves rolled up, I would search his arms and eyes for telltale signs of drug use. It was just something that I did. But every search brought about the reassurance that he was okay. There had been no needle marks. No pupil irregularities. Not a word would be spoken because, as far as I could tell, there was nothing for me to worry about. As far as I could tell, he was safe.

I already was aware, at this stage, that Peter had tried cannabis a few years earlier. Since then, rather than keep asking questions which I felt would alienate him, I thought it wiser to just use my eyes and ears.

During his first few weeks at university, we had met for lunch at the home of Nanny London. The kids had always called my mother Nanny Liverpool and my husband's mother Nanny London. He couldn't wait to tell us all about his experimentation – we'd always had an open rapport; an honesty. So he and I went for a walk and a two-hour chat ensued.

I went mad.

'Everyone smokes it,' he told me.

'And that makes it right?' I argued. He hadn't a leg to stand on.

Hadn't I always told him it was a 'gateway drug'? Not every cannabis user goes on to take hard drugs, but statistics show that most hard-drug users began by smoking cannabis. 'Mum!' he scoffed. 'I'd never take heroin!'

Famous last words.

Peter had left home not smoking. Nanny Liverpool had smoked and he'd detested it. He didn't like even to sit in the same room if she was having a cigarette. He'd won a local poetry award with a poem about smoking. 'Cough cough cough,' he'd written. 'Coughing up what shouldn't have been there in the first place'. He'd won a cash prize, too – and now here he was, keen to share his rebellion with me.

I was grateful for our long talk and honestly really felt I'd made an impact. How foolish mothers can be. He was nineteen and away from home.

My son was now a smoker. Happily, in front of me, it was only cigars or cigarettes from a packet (I noticed, suitably relieved). Nowadays, I hardly ever see him without a cigarette in his hand, whether he's performing or on a television interview.

To think I used to be concerned about *cigarettes*.

'Smoking'

cough cough cough
coughing up what shouldn't have been there in the first place.
a cloud lifts my eyes, then drags them down,
then does what it pleases.

my mum would like to know why I bother.
so would I.
even it was only one.
taken from a packet swept off a glass and bottle topped
    table as
the previous owner staggered to his home. Or to the toilet.
his manner suggested one and the same.

a famous brand. A week before I'd
managed another half full
    half empty
packet. On the floor. Shining at me.
so, in total, a full pack.
fagging marvellous.

that's all well and clever,
but sat on a cold window white ledge
at not quite nearly midnight,
coughing it up, wetness in vision,
wondering if I'm quite all there after all,
it's not all well and clever. Don't like it.
but then, much as I don't like the actual, it,
I like it, as an idea.
I'd like to like it.

mates all smoke,
grandparents, dad will soon, he says.
used to.

little orange and white pipe of puff.
worth its weight in tar
or something.
cough it up, and never will again.
it gives me no pleasure.
and has nothing to do with
[as none of it does, none of us do],
campaigns.
of any kind.
Peter Doherty, July 1996

By January, my mother had become quite unwell. In the spring Peter flew to Japan to tour with the band The Libertines but, towards the end of the tour, his nan's condition deteriorated rapidly and, in April 2003, she died. Despite being a military family, all the children were very close to all their grandparents and Peter flew in from Japan to attend the funeral in Liverpool. He had been very busy since we had last met for the family Christmas some four months before and, although we had spoken on the phone, I hadn't seen him. After the funeral, he was scheduled to join the rest of the band in New York.

I had driven from Germany to England, stopping off to collect Emily from school. AmyJo met us in London at my mother-in-law's house where we all stayed overnight, awaiting Peter's arrival early next morning. Of course, he was late. This is a usual feature of his behaviour beginning with when he was born when he'd kept us all waiting for two whole long weeks. But I do have to add that, much of the time when he is late, it isn't his fault! I've often remarked to him that – given the absolute and never-ending demands that create chaos in his day-to-day life – Shakespeare himself could write no more complex a plot: there are always extenuating circumstances involved (and plenty of irony). But, this time, the poor chap had crossed continents to be with the family and so a few hours weren't a problem.

Eventually, he arrived and, immediately, I sensed the unease within him but put it down to jet lag and the fact he had not seen his nanny to say goodbye. He was a sensitive soul and had enjoyed a special relationship with Nanny Liverpool. Since we were all grieving anyway, we weren't too perturbed by Peter's reactions and made allowances for his obviously fragile state of mind.

I drove the family to Liverpool for the funeral. In the car, we laughed and cried as we remembered all the moments we had shared with my mother. Everyone giggled as we recalled the time when a young Peter, on an overnight visit to Liverpool, had risen early, spotted his nan's false teeth in the bathroom and had tried them out for size. (One of the many *innocent* family sensations Peter has caused over the years.) It was a sight we'll never forget. 'Perhaps nanny has left you her teeth in her will,' I joked.

By the time we reached Liverpool, his behaviour was noticeably strange. He was tearful, melancholic, not the Peter we knew – but, to be honest, there was too much to do to pay him a lot of attention. Although he was well dressed, he was tired and fidgety but, I kept telling myself, he had just flown in from Japan, so it was to be expected. It was a very painful time for everyone.

All the way up to Liverpool, Peter had been bemoaning the fact that he only had a pair of brown shoes with him. 'I don't think nanny minds what colour shoes you wear,' I told him; but, being fastidious about his appearance, it was a constant source of worry for him. To be absolutely truthful, there was nothing in his manner that rang alarm bells at this time. I suspected nothing at this point. It is only in retrospect that these details have become important. I remember that I kept looking at him in the car on the drive up as he slept in the front passenger seat beside me. My mother had just died. I was trying hard to keep it all together. I wanted just to cry and cry but felt that I had to keep it all together for the children. We were all hurting very much. I wasn't too concerned over Peter but made a mental note to ensure that we had some time to talk when the opportunity arose over the next day or so. There was nothing that I could put my finger on . . . it was just a feeling. One of those nagging 'mother' feelings.

When we arrived in Liverpool, we went as a family to pay our respects to my mother in the chapel of rest. Even this solemn occasion was filled with love and laughter and memories of how we had gathered in the very same place, just four years earlier, at my dad's coffin-side to pay our last respects. Then, my mother had almost fainted as she looked inside the coffin. She had been married to my dad for fifty-seven years but didn't recognise him at all. 'It's not your dad, it's not Percy!' The reason for this was that dad's moustache had been shaved! In fifty-seven years she had only ever seen him with a moustache. How we had all laughed, it was so funny. Now, back in the same place, there was a twist to the tale; as we gathered all around we were aghast to see that my mum, indeed, had hair around her mouth! All we could say was that she had my dad's moustache!

There was so much to prepare for the following day. Eventually, AmyJo, Emily and I went to get our hair done in town but Peter wanted to sleep, so we left him. On our return, he was still sleeping but, shortly before 7 p.m., he woke and began worrying about his footwear again – and the fact he didn't have a black tie. Somebody said there was an Asda store nearby so Peter and I headed off to see if we could buy what he needed.

Once inside the store, he picked up two white shirts, a black tie, a black suit, and a beautiful pair of black leather shoes that was only £16 – so cheap that I asked the assistant, 'How much for two?' Peter nudged me and said, 'By George it's good at Asda.' As we passed through the checkout, I asked if he'd like a coffee. It seemed a perfect time to have a chat. It would have been nice to just have a one-to-one with him; to spend some time with my grown son. All mothers feel this I think. But the café had just closed so we made our way back to the car park. En route, we passed two young men who said: ''Ey, that's one of the lead singers out of The Libertines isn't it?' Peter asked if I'd heard them. I said 'Yes, were they talking about me?'

As we sat in the car outside his uncle's house, Peter told me he had a problem. He told me he was fragile and began to unfold his innermost feelings. He began to skirt around the fact that the words of his songs were about drugs, I was shocked. I felt he was about to tell me something momentous. I asked whether he was unhappy – but suddenly we were interrupted by a family member who had seen us pull up outside.

All sorts of things were rushing around my heart and my head. I wanted to tell the person who'd interrupted us to go away, that we were busy. The moment was lost. There was no chance now to pin him down. We all headed to a local hostelry and Peter's normal, charismatic self seemed to have come back, if only for a short while. I knew, now, that something serious was unfolding but was still unaware of the extent of his problems, his fears and his demons.

I couldn't settle, torn between grief for my dead mother and utter panic for my troubled son.

The following morning, a beautiful wreath arrived, expressing condolences from Rough Trade records and the rest of the band, which really touched my heart. It was a lovely gesture and Peter was touched by it as well.

Peter senior was due to be arriving from Germany, so I went to collect him from the airport after leaving Peter with family and friends. He seemed to have pulled himself together well. He was back on form and entertaining everyone without any sign of his previous concerns. Following a moving funeral service, in which Peter was a pall-bearer, all seemed as well as could be expected; and, whilst I was busy greeting extended family, Peter and his father slipped away for a walk and a chat along the estuary at Hale, outside Liverpool. I never asked what had passed between them.

Quite unbeknown to me, then, were my husband's worries about Peter's behaviour. Initially Peter senior used the web to keep up with the band's progress. It was a source of pride to read the band's own website. He had followed with excitement as the band had developed and as it received more airplay, bigger write-ups and even small mentions in the national press. But he quickly became concerned about what he was reading. He scrutinised other web sites constantly, and read all the stories online about Peter's emerging troubles, but he didn't disclose any of his concerns to me at that time. He tried to shield me from the reality of the situation, hoping that it was all just hype and that it would sort itself out soon enough. He believed that Peter's strong sense of family would prevent him from being too wild.

This was rock'n'roll. This was what youngsters did. But his Peter, he felt, would never follow in the well-trodden steps of the many that had gone before. Now, his world was slowly falling apart as he watched his potentially gifted son spiral out of control.

Of course, there were the odd articles in the media that I saw, too; but, at the time, we had thought there was no such thing as bad publicity. We knew that most of what Peter was reported as saying in interviews was completely untrue – he loved making things up for journalists – so it just seemed natural to assume that these reports were not true, either. We were living in a different country, in a different culture and, compared to Peter, in a different world.

It seems a silly thing to say, but it had been a lovely day at the funeral: the family together, wonderful memories flooding back – and catching up with long-lost neighbours. We'd planned to stay late and take Peter to Heathrow to catch his flight to New York. Life goes on.

AmyJo, a teacher in south London, had to be at work the following day, and Emily had to be back at her boarding school because exams were looming. But, as the day passed, Peter became increasingly anxious to return to London that night and was prepared to make his own way to Heathrow. AmyJo was concerned because he'd told her he didn't really want to go to America. By late afternoon/early evening, therefore, we were all packed and on our way to London. She was worried that he might miss his flight unless we took him to Heathrow direct.

It was obvious that Peter was not at ease. He was irritable, saying strange things and asking repeatedly how long it would be before we arrived in London. He kept asking and asking. It seemed so important to him. He specifically wanted to be dropped off in Whitechapel. He refused to go to his sister's flat. It had to be Whitechapel – he *had* to meet someone, but he didn't say whom. I can't remember if we asked whom it was he was so eager to meet, it was really none of our business. He was an adult and didn't have to keep us informed of whom he wanted to meet.

We stopped off at a motorway service station for coffee and refreshments. This upset him; such was his desire to reach London. He did eat and have a drink but I can remember feeling uncomfortable in his company for probably the first time in my life. We'd never experienced any 'Kevin the teenager' years with Peter; he had been a wonderful child growing up, so happy, so funny, so much a part of the family. We missed him when he left home. I miss him now.

This young man was not a person I was familiar with. There were glimpses of the Peter I knew but they were only fleeting. Of course, he'd grown up – it happens – he had a mind of his own now. But there were no jokes. Peter and his dad usually had a repartee – they could quote anything from 'Hancock' to 'Only Fools and Horses' and talk for hours about football, especially their beloved QPR. But this banter was conspicuous by its absence. He had no interest in holding a conversation with anyone.

And so it was that we drove to Whitechapel – myself, my husband, Emily and AmyJo – lost in our own concerns for

Peter. Silently, grappling with the truth that we were wanting so much to deny . . . the rumours we'd read in the *NME* regarding missed performances, band disputes, the lyrics to his songs and the innuendoes they contained. On The Libertines' first album, the refrain for the song 'Horror Show' was about the 'horse' being 'brown'. 'Horse' was slang for heroin – as was 'brown'. Although it is hard to expand on clues that we'd seen, there was nothing concrete at this point. However, the truth that Peter was dabbling – and more – with drugs was beginning to dawn on us.

Back in the sixties, with my school friends, I used to listen to lyrics of songs like 'Lucy in the Sky with Diamonds'. In the playground we would say, 'That's about LSD.' And I remember much later singing the LA's song 'There She Goes', not realising it was about drugs. I felt confused: why would Peter be writing songs about heroin?

He needed to see someone in Whitechapel that night, all right – someone who could get what he needed most at this time. Not the comfort or the love of his family, not the tour that lay ahead, but someone who could supply his need for drugs. I can't describe the pain, mainly because I was numb. I reminded myself that he had NO needle marks. 'It was probably cannabis,' I told myself.

We were a family that coped. We were problem solvers. But I knew this one was going to be a toughie.

Drugs and illegal activity are an anathema to me. I'm a God, Queen and Country person. Never smoked, never tried drugs, always liked to be in control of my own mind but, now, I felt that I was losing my mind. The grieving process that should have been beginning for the loss of my mother had been usurped by growing panic for my son.

As we dropped him off in Whitechapel, well dressed, fedora in situ, we cried silently to ourselves, unable to face that dark, innermost realisation that Peter was, in fact, taking drugs. Hard drugs. Life-destroying drugs. We remained silent. We had a sixteen-year-old girl in the car who, we hoped, was oblivious to everything, so we couldn't ask Peter any questions. Plus we were in shock. It was unbelievable. Peter disappeared into the night.

Once Peter had left us, the atmosphere in the car was estranged. We tried to chat, but couldn't find the words to encourage each other. Very quickly, it seemed, we arrived at AmyJo's place. As her bags were being unloaded AmyJo threw her arms around me and cried and cried. Not for her nanny, but for her brother. As we held each other she told me that he was in trouble. But Emily was still around and she didn't elaborate. We were all too scared, too shocked, too worried to speak openly, although it wasn't the Doherty norm to be quiet when some comment was required.

That he managed to make his flight to New York brought enormous relief when I found out the following day. Perhaps, just perhaps, my fears were an over-reaction. He had said he didn't want to go to America but the band was out there waiting for him. So, whatever it was that he wanted to stay for in London obviously wasn't that important any more. Oh! the things we can convince ourselves of.

*

Looking back at that night, I don't know how I coped – but probably the same way as I do today. I pray a lot. Incessantly, in fact. But we must be careful what we pray for because we may just get it. My initial prayers for Peter were: 'If only I could just get him to rehab.' But it turned out rehab wasn't the answer. Six rehabs later, it is fair to say that my prayers have changed.

A friend I've known for many years, Barbara, sent me a book that was to sustain me daily, and still does. It's called *Prodigals – and Those Who Love Them*. The author is Ruth Bell Graham who is the wife of American evangelist Billy Graham.

The dictionary definition of prodigal is 'somebody who is recklessly wasteful or extravagant'. A prodigal son or daughter is a child who has left the family home to lead their own life in a reckless way. The parable of the Prodigal Son is about such a son, but one who returns repentant. The author is a mother of five children, two of whom were prodigals.

If you have a child away from the family fold, or know of anyone worrying or fretting over their child – or even if you're simply concerned about another human being – then I fully commend this book to you. I have bought several copies, now, and have given them to other grieving mothers. It doesn't really matter if you believe in God or not when you read this hope-giving book. It will strengthen you when you have no strength, it will give you hope where there may be none, it will empower you to put one foot in front of the other when all you want to do is lay down and die.

The author reminds the reader of the hurt and disappointment of the one wandering and understands only too well the confusion and fear of the one who waits for the wanderer's return.

It's balm to a hurting heart. I hope this book does the same for aching hearts everywhere.

Chapter 2

Fear Knocks at the Door

Terra incognita – Unknown ground

FROM THE DAY of Nanny Liverpool's funeral to Peter's first rehab was eight weeks. Eight weeks of madness in Peter's life. In those eight weeks Peter, my husband, had received a new posting and we had moved from Germany to Holland. This would be our first experience of living in the Netherlands and we were looking forward to it. Once again, we were living in a border town, a beautiful place called Sittard which bordered Germany. However, my husband would be working some twenty minutes away in the magnificent city of Maastricht. This was going to be an exciting adventure for us and we had such plans to make the very best of the new posting.

We have been married almost thirty years and have moved many times. Before I married, I, too, had served in the Army as a nurse for six years and had experienced several moves. Since our marriage, though, we have moved from our first home together in Aldershot on to Ouston, Catterick, Krefeld (West Germany as it was then) Northern Ireland, Cyprus, Krefeld (Germany, since the Berlin wall came down) Blandford, Bramcote (near Nuneaton) Krefeld (third time!), Wildenrath, Sittard and Blandford (again). That's a lot of packing and unpacking! That's a lot of fun. That's a lot of friends. A wonderful life.

Obviously, Peter had been given our new address – numerous times – and, because he was always losing his phone, I had ensured that all those around him were able to contact me, day or night.

One week after moving, almost eight weeks since the funeral, the inevitable call came whilst I was on night duty: it was someone very close to Peter and the band calling to tell me that he was way out of control; that someone now needed to take control, someone needed to be taking responsibility for him and his ever-increasing, drug-induced frenzies. Parental intervention was now required and they told me of the many problems that the band and all those around them had to endure due to Peter's drug taking. The relationship, they said, was now untenable. Untenable? Drug-induced frenzies? What the hell were they talking about? Late for rehearsals . . . Mood swings . . . Bizarre behaviour . . . Why hadn't I heard this before? Why had they left it until now to say parental intervention was required?

What did I know? Peter had left home years before!

What could I do? Where would I begin? I didn't even know where he lived. According to the papers he had lived in, and just been evicted from, the 'Albion' rooms! He and a few others had set sail (not literally) on an Albion adventure into Arcadia. Albion is an archaic Celtic word for 'England' or Britain. Arcadia, I had learnt, was a place of simple rustic contentment. Apart from the boys in the band – with whom, I was now being told, he had strained relationships – I didn't know who else was around him.

How was he going to react to his mother turning up to spoil his fun?

I wanted to faint; to stop them talking; to shout: 'Why has it got so far without anyone calling me?' But instead . . . perhaps I said that I was sorry, but I can't remember. I assured them I'd be on the first possible plane to London. I just packed a small bag. I was trying to maintain calmness so I could establish all the facts. Everything was beginning to add up – his bizarre behaviour back in Liverpool . . . but, even though the jigsaw was coming together, I still found it completely impossible to believe.

A meeting had been set up for that very afternoon as I arrived – a rendezvous with the management of Rough Trade, the band's record label, who were based on the Golborne Road in West London. As I walked there from the tube station, my heart pounded with the fear of what I would have to face but, as soon as I arrived, three very kind people met me to give advice and comfort: Geoff Travis and Jeanette Lee who ran the label, and James Endeacott who was Rough Trade's A&R man. We were later joined by AmyJo and a heavily pregnant Lisa Moorish – lead singer with the band Kill City – who was expecting Peter's child (my first grandchild).

Of all the things that were said by these very know-ledgeable people, one of them I have recalled many times because it has turned out to be so true. Geoff Travis was talking about rehabilitation and recovery when he said: 'In two or three years, when Peter is over this . . .', the implication being that it would take that long for Peter to get back on track.

Two or three years? I wanted to argue – protest – as he spoke, but didn't, my manners getting the better of me. This was unbelievable! Having had no experience of drug problems, it never even occurred to me that, once it had been identified, there would still be two or three years before the problem was resolved. And that turned out to be the major issue for me – that these things take time. In fact, three years have come and gone and Peter's still not back on track. I've since learned that three years for many alcoholics or addicts is, sadly, just the beginning; it can take many, many years for recovery to be a reality – if they recover at all.

They were so kind to me – this silly, middle-aged mum from Ivory Towers – in meeting to discuss the best way forward to tackle the Peter Problem.

Fortuitously, Peter called Lisa during the meeting and

told her where he was and it wasn't long before we – myself, AmyJo, and Lisa, along with my first grandchild in utero – were on our way to find him.

I remember both girls begging me not to go in to the hotel – that they would assess the situation and come and get me – but I insisted. Whatever I had to face, it didn't matter. All I knew was that the truth had to be faced. I had no idea why they were so worried, and thought that, for them to be so anxious, they must have seen him in some bad way that I hadn't. I braced myself for the worst.

A polite Polish hotel clerk rang Peter's room to say his sister and two others were there to see him (he wasn't expecting us and the girls were afraid there could be trouble). Since Peter had three people in his room already, the clerk told him some would have to leave. I can only assume Peter had said 'No problem,' because, seconds later, he appeared on the stairs saying goodbye to three people and spotted me. 'Mum!' he said, hugging, kissing me and picking me up; he seemed genuinely pleased to see me. More importantly, he looked fine.

We followed him upstairs and my eyes scanned his room, searching for any evidence of drug use. I couldn't see anything to cause concern. Peter was smart, clean, lucid and his eyes seemed okay. In fact, to be honest I couldn't understand what all the fuss was about. The room was *very* Peter – a canopied bed in a rich, red décor. Very poetic.

After some time had elapsed, I asked if I could visit his bathroom – there was bound to be trouble lurking in there (that's how it goes in the films anyway). Peter never turned a hair at my desire to use his loo and, once inside, I searched high and low but couldn't find a thing – not even a pair of sunglasses.

Eventually, he got around to asking why I was in London and what I was doing in the hotel. Slowly, gently, I began to unfold the events from the phone call the previous night up to my arrival. As we sat on his bed, bonding and talking, I asked him about his fragility – a word he often used to describe himself – and his drug taking. I told him to be honest with me – that there was no point in lying – and I asked him if he was injecting heroin.

At first, there was a weak denial – to himself, really, rather than to me. Then it all came out. He was smoking heroin and crack cocaine.

Smoking heroin and crack cocaine.

I can't explain how I felt. I can't.

I was mortified. I wanted to hit him. I wanted to be sick; to be deaf; to be struck down; to hold him; to cry out to God.

No wonder there were no needle marks – my son was *smoking* heroin. I remember thanking God for that small mercy – which may seem a bit odd but it took me back to a book I had read called *The Hiding Place* by a Dutch woman called Corrie ten Boom. Her family turned her home into a refuge for fugitives from the Nazis during World War II. Later, she and other members of her family were taken to various concentration camps and only she returned alive.

However, she never lost her faith despite the atrocities she experienced – and she even thanked God when she had lice! She and her sister, like many in the concentration camps, had lice and were so very ashamed and shuddered to think what their mother would think; but it had turned out that having lice as they did had actually saved them from some worse fate by keeping the guards out of the huts.

I hope those reading this book will never find themselves in the position I am now in with my son. If you do – or you already are – please don't lose sight of the fact that we never know what tomorrow will bring. I remember being so proud of my children who were bright, upright citizens. They would never take drugs or break the law; they were past their teenage years and we'd sailed through those without a hitch. Hadn't I watched other parents who'd had awful trouble with their kids? Hadn't I felt smug?

Pride cometh before a fall.

My small mercy at that time, I had foolishly thought, was that if he was smoking heroin it was somehow not as bad as injecting it. Naivety. Uninformed. Ignorance.

I didn't shout at Peter. We talked and talked for hours, his phone ringing incessantly, the hotel clerk forever calling up to say various people wanted to see him. One person – a music manager Peter knew – was allowed to come up for a few minutes and attempted to persuade Peter to go to Italy with him. He was trying to 'sort Peter out'. Many, so many, have tried.

Over the years there have been countless people, famous and unknown, who have tried very hard, and really given of themselves, to avail Peter of the help he requires. As a mother, sometimes it's very hard to watch people trying to help. Each person thinks they have the answer. More often than not, when people offer help, I'm so grateful and feel that they may indeed have the answer. Sadly, the reality is that only Peter can help himself.

We all cried and spoke of rehab and, eventually, when everyone was exhausted, it came time to leave him. Peter seemed so keen to 'do the right thing'; it all seemed so easy that it was difficult to see a problem at this stage. Bless him, he was still reading avidly – one of his earlier visitors had brought him, at his behest, some books. Lisa stayed on a while after we left and I felt confident things could only get better. The following day someone rang me from Rough Trade with great news. Peter was on his way to rehab!

He was taken to a treatment and care centre called Farm Place in a beautiful part of Surrey. I couldn't believe it. It was so easy. Why hadn't they tried this tack before? I thanked them profusely and remember asking if they could make sure that Peter had a pen and paper and some classics to read. Peter writes in his journal every day and has done since he was a child. Wherever he is, you can be sure that a pen or pencil and definitely a book won't be very far away. I couldn't tell you what he wrote – I have never read any of his journals. This is a hard one, for any parent, as there's a part of you that would always like to pick up a child's journal and read it, but it never crossed my mind to pick up Peter's. In the past, there was never any cause — he was always so well behaved. By this point, Peter had been living away from home for four years so there wouldn't have been an opportunity, anyway.

With Peter safely on his way to rehab — and no visitors allowed until we were given the go ahead — I returned to Holland. The news was encouraging and, when I spoke to him, I assured him that I would visit just as soon as I was allowed. Apparently he hadn't had any withdrawal symptoms and I took this to be 'good' news. This obviously meant that he wasn't an addict — everyone had just been overreacting, right? Wrong. But I never sought an explanation for this non-withdrawal.

I offered to compile a potted history of his life for the rehab staff in case it would help in any way with the wider picture. I wasn't sure who would use it but I found it therapeutic. It took four hours to collate everything — poems, photos, etc. — and then the phone rang. It was Farm Place. Peter had just discharged himself and was on his way back to London — with no money.

He'd been there just under a week before he decided to run away. We'd only been in our new home in Sittard for a couple of weeks and I was in the middle of hanging my curtains at the house's huge front window — all Dutch houses have huge windows. I had to leave metres and metres of curtains on the dining-room table and, instead, pack my bag and book a ticket for the Channel Tunnel. I phoned my husband, who was at work in Maastricht, to tell him what had happened and that I was on my way to England. He listened. At first there was silence. Then, 'Take care, drive safely,' he said.

Recently, I have been able to ask my husband how he had felt during these times – the phone calls and the to-ing and the fro-ing. I even broached the hitherto unasked question of why he had never come with me. It was a moment of honesty. It was something that I had feared asking, not wanting to hurt an already hurting human being, especially not wanting to hurt someone that I loved and wanted so much to protect.

The truth, as hard as it is to hear, is always the best answer. He told me that he had been relieved that I was going to England and had felt strongly that was where I should be. But he also felt completely unable to come with me; he knew that he would get angry and the bottom line was that he had no strength to face the awfulness of the situation.

Why had I never asked before? Fear. Fear of hurting, Fear of hearing what you already know.

Fear knocked at the door.

Faith answered.

No one was there.

And so I set off in the car to England. It was a frenetic drive – six hours to London via Holland, Belgium and France. My mobile phone was ringing constantly beside me on the seat.

I was desperate to answer it in case it was news from Peter or from anyone around him. Eventually I had to stop to check the phone and find out if anybody had spotted him.

It was such a shock that he had left the rehab centre – the obvious answer to his problems. Why would he leave somewhere that was designed to help him? I just couldn't understand it.

Everyone was waiting for him to surface. The logistics of finding him were complex. Ringing here. Ringing there. But it wasn't too long before I tracked him down. He was safe, he assured me: 'clean' (by now drug slang was used in everyday conversation); 'didn't have a problem' (denial); and, yes, he would meet me in Soho tomorrow. 'Don't worry, mum,' he said.

Surprisingly, he turned up on time and he looked great. He was still absent without leave from Farm Place but they were holding his bed. This was another of those awkward times. What could I say? 'You naughty boy' . . . 'You fool'? And it was another of those times when a sense of humour sneaks in; before I could utter a word of disparagement, there I was singing, 'How you gonna keep 'em down on the farm?'

We embraced. It was a time for talking, not for shouting.

We sat and drank coffee on the pavement at a corner café in Soho, awaiting the arrival of his older sister. It seemed that every second person knew him and we were interrupted many times for autographs or a chance 'Hello!' Peter was so patient with everyone, so kind, so gentle with them and with me. Finally, he agreed to return to the rehab centre. I would go with him, there and then, in a taxi. I phoned Rough Trade. 'Yes! Go, go!' they said. I phoned Farm Place; it was quite some distance away and would take a few hours to get there. 'No problem – come, come.'

During the second phone call, a fellow songster had arrived with guitar in tow and he and Peter began to strum and sing. Within minutes, the pavement was crowded with people, spilling over into the road. Some were singing. Some were waiting for autographs. My heart sank. Suddenly the moment was lost and, as Peter came to his next song, he intimated with his doe-eyed look that this was where he wanted to be.

He wouldn't be returning to rehab after all.

I felt desolate. That's the only word I can use to describe how I was feeling. A bed was being held, the taxi was on its way but, with a few notes plucked on a guitar, my hope that Peter would return to the only place that could help him was destroyed.

Eventually we were joined by AmyJo and spent the whole day together around Soho, having lunch in one of Peter's favourite restaurants. It was a good day; there was no evidence of any drugs and no sloping off anywhere. I'd been told he didn't have any withdrawal symptoms and, because he didn't feel the need to slope off, I talked myself into thinking there might not actually be a problem. Maybe he was just a recreational drug user. I asked him to return with me to Nanny London's house but, when he looked back into my eyes, he told me that he loved me but that he couldn't come with me.

In that moment I knew that yes, he loved me, but that he loved something else much, much more. This is one moment I'll never forget. It was so hard to leave him. I cried all the way to his nan's house.

That same Saturday, The Libertines were playing a big gig – I think it was the Glastonbury Festival – and Peter was devastated that he couldn't join them. I often think that's why he left rehab, to join his band mates at that gig. He was genuinely shocked and traumatised that they'd play without him. He just couldn't see that he'd left them no choice. Although there were problems at this time, they were still a band.

I had left him late that night and he said he would meet me the next day, but the following morning I couldn't get hold of him. I tried the next day, too, but to no avail. When we eventually spoke, he said he was very busy, playing with some different people and 'keeping out of trouble'.

Over the next few weeks I travelled – many, many times – back and forth, to and from London, either by plane or car. I found myself in strange places, mixing with people who led very different lifestyles to mine. Some of these people had strange names, too, and even stranger habits. But, if I wanted to keep some line of communication open with my evasive son, then I needed to accommodate his friends. There were, it seemed, hundreds of them.

'No, haven't seen him today, try . . .' It was very hard to keep track of Peter. This was the summer of discontent – the first of several to come. Who would have imagined that so much could have happened in such a short space of time? And it was even harder to imagine how many rehabs there would be.

After that first rehab in June 2003, it would be nearly a year until the second in May 2004. Then, they would follow in quick succession. A third in May–June 2004 and then a fourth in June 2004. Three in just one month. February 2005 would see the fifth rehab and the first implant (an implant helps prevent heroin from taking effect). With a second implant following in July 2005. The sixth rehab would come in November 2005. To avoid confusion, and to set the record straight, here are the dates.

1   Rehab June 2003 (England)
2   Rehab May 2004 (England)
3   Rehab May–June 2004 (England)
4   Rehab June 2004 (Thailand)
5   Rehab February 2005 and first implant (England)
     Second implant July 2005 (England)
6   Rehab November 2005 (America)

I won't even attempt to chart all the court cases or the remands that Peter has had as there are far too many and lots of them overlap – in a word, it is all very confusing. But it would be fair to say that, since Christmas 2002, the Peter

Problem has been constant. There is rarely a moment when I am not thinking about, or working on, the Peter Problem.

On one such visit to the UK to track Peter down, I was dashing across to Earl's Court to meet Peter when, as I entered the tube, was surprised to see some old neighbours of mine from Germany. Usually the chatty one, I could hardly speak. I felt apoplectic and didn't want anyone to see me. What if they were alighting at the same station as me? Could they tell that I had the weight of the world on my shoulders? Thankfully, I disembarked first. In a few short months they would know. The whole world would know.

This meeting was very sad. Peter was extremely fragile, tearful, remorseful. We walked around a graveyard; he was in a dreadful state. 'How have things got to this?' he said aloud. I begged him to let me get him help, pleaded with him to go to another rehab and stick at it this time.

He lay on the ground in the graveyard. I don't know why he lay there. Physically, he could walk. He seemed just to want to lie down, not in a tired way – perhaps in an attempt to rid himself of his agony. I didn't know what to do. I looked down at him lying on the ground. I wasn't sure if he had taken anything, but presumed he had. I sat down beside him. Eventually, after talking to him, he seemed to momentarily pull himself together. Although it was a very hot, very beautiful summer's day, he was keen to have my opinion on the trench coat that he had bought in America.

I told him that we couldn't stay here all day and suggested that we go and see his sister AmyJo who was already expecting us. He agreed. I managed to get him across London to his sister's house in a cab; he slept almost all of the way. The taxi driver asked if he was okay. 'No,' I replied. 'He's ill, very ill indeed.'

When Peter woke up, hours later, he seemed like a different person. I found this difficult to understand. At the time, I knew very little about drugs and their effect. I had imagined that he would wake up and want more drugs but, in fact, this wasn't the case. He was starving hungry, eating everything in sight, having a laugh. Ah, the old Peter had returned for the afternoon.

But a few hours later he had to leave us and get back to the band.

Always, at this point of him leaving, in my heart and head there is a great battle. Invisible tears flow, inaudible prayers are thrown heavenward. I call upon his Guardian Angel to protect him, and for the Holy Spirit to touch his heart and show him a better way. I cover him in prayer from head to toe. I feel, very much, as though I'm in a spiritual battle for the soul of my son. I have lost many of these 'battles'. But the war is not over yet.

Who else in the whole wide world will pray for him? Isn't this what mothers do? Peter is lucky. His sister and Nanny London pray too. This may be why the press refers to me wrongly as a Catholic, because I am neither ashamed nor embarrassed to admit that I have a deep faith.

At these points of leaving, as my heart-and-head battles

begin and, while the Christian in me would have peace, the worldly me wants to lash out, wants to tie Peter up and prevent him from leaving – knowing, as I do, where he will go and what he will do when he leaves. If I could just lock him up for a few months . . .

I knew what was best. *I* was his mother. *I* could keep him on the straight and narrow.

Don't we hear things many times in life, Christian or not, about God and 'free will', and don't we dismiss it or take it on board according to our own beliefs? But, in these moments, I have become acutely aware of 'free will' in relation to the parable of the Prodigal Son, whose loving father allowed him to leave, despite knowing it was not best for him. He never clobbered him over the head to make him stay. God allows us our free will, our choice, and remains steadfast awaiting our return. He doesn't turn us into automatons. He never prevents us from leaving Him and He is constantly alert to our call for help at any time, no matter where we are or how deep in sin.

And so, yes, at these times of departing, I have allowed my son to walk freely away. In these moments, many times, in my hidden grief and utter sorrow, my heart has felt the great love that God has for each of us. I had to let go and let God.

Chapter 3

A Baby . . . and a Shambles

Abyssus, abyssum – Hell calls hell:
one misstep leads to another

AMID ALL THE mayhem and mess and misery of the past three years there was, however, one big, bright, bubbly and joyful event. It was an event that, had we had the time to think about it, we perhaps would have preferred not to have happened; but, while I was chasing Peter from pillar to post, his unborn child was growing and, on 13 July 2003, baby Astile arrived.

He was a big (8lb 5oz), beautiful baby. Peter was at the hospital throughout the birth, as was his big sister AmyJo. Peter senior and I were in Holland and awaited the news of a safe delivery with excited anticipation, tinged of course, with sadness, knowing that this little mite was entering the world to meet an addicted daddy.

However imperfect the circumstances were, this little

darling boy has brought much joy and laughter where there was none. He alone, I believe, has given his grandad a raison d'être. To see a fully grown roughie toughie, ex-airborne soldier playing sword fighting (using large twigs) with a tot beneath a huge tree in Hyde Park, shouting 'Bish, bash, bosh', brings cheer to a nanna's heart and memories flooding back of twenty-five years earlier when the same roughie toughie was doing the same thing with his own son. Except for the fact that grandad was no longer so fleet of foot, I would have been convinced it was little Peter under that tree, such is the likeness.

Naturally, we don't see as much of Astile as we would like to – what grandparent does? But he has our blood in him and the whole family loves him. The cupboards are full of toys for him and grandad has, to date, bought no less than three train sets. This child (did I mention that he is a natural with a football?) has done more to heal my husband's heart than any medicine could.

Astile reminds me of his daddy when he was that age. Let's hope that he doesn't remind me of his dad when he's twenty-seven! Astile is adored by his aunties – Peter's sisters – and, in some small way, I suppose we all feel that, by showing our love for Peter's son, we are actually showing our love for him.

I travelled to England a lot during the August of 2003 to try to see Peter. Babyshambles, the other band that he was playing with while there were difficulties with The Libertines, was due to play a gig at The Troubadour Club in the Old Brompton Road on 22 August. Sat on a sidewalk on a hot summer's night in the heart of Kensington and Chelsea's bohemian quarter, a nanny (Nanny London – my mother-in-law) in her mid-seventies, a distressed mother in her fifties (me) and an impressionable teenage sister (Emily) waited patiently.

It was far too early to be there – only 7.30 p.m. Peter wouldn't be performing until much later; but we each felt that, if we arrived early, then there was some small chance of being able to meet up with him, although for what reason probably none of us could say. We sat there in the hope of seeing him with our own eyes (a chance for me to check his arms for evidence of needle marks). The venue had sounded decent and a place we could all go to. Initially, I had wanted to go alone – it's easy to forget that other people love him, too. There was no way that I would be able to leave my mother-in-law and daughter behind – they wouldn't hear of it. Either we all went, or nobody did.

We'd crossed London in a taxi. None of us really knew what to wear, realising that whatever we did wear would be wholly inappropriate. We felt and looked like an unlikely bunch of gig-going misfits. But this was not about us; this was about someone in the family who was an addict. We could have worn sky-blue pink pyjamas and it wouldn't have mattered. Peter had been told that we were coming and had said that he'd try to see us beforehand, and that was good enough for us: we knew we had to be there.

I had travelled earlier that day from Holland to the UK

to try to see Peter and also to see my grandson Astile, who was just six-and-a-half-weeks old by this time. The following day, Emily and I were supposed to be going to the Reading Festival to see the rest of The Libertines, with whom I still had contact, but this night we were only concerned with seeing Peter. Hanging over all our heads was the fact that Peter had, shortly after Astile's birth, been arrested and charged with burglary after allegedly breaking into the flat of his long-time band-mate Carl Barât. The impending court case was scheduled for 8 September – just over two weeks away.

There was an ambiguity of feelings in all our hearts; impatient to see Peter yet dreading it, but there we were sat on the sidewalk outside The Troubadour. Very quickly the venue filled up and all sorts of recognisable faces were sitting around us. It was a very nice location. The doors didn't open until 8 p.m. and Peter wasn't on until 10 p.m. Astile's mum, Lisa Moorish, had joined us and introduced us to so many people. I was impressed! The atmosphere was amazing – full of warmth, excitement and expectation. By about 9 p.m., the place was awash with people. There was no longer any room inside the venue, and people were posing and jostling outside on the sidewalk.

I had interesting conversations with a variety of people, from film directors and bodyguards to actors and journalists, and always, as is my wont, I asked succinctly if they took drugs. If the answer was yes, I'd ask why, how, and what they took. Nowadays, I include the question: 'What was the first drug you ever used?' Almost always the answer is cannabis.

Peter arrived and the waiting crowd erupted. Girls asked for his autograph, took pictures on their phones; boys asked for the same. We had all of two minutes to talk to him – enough time for me to scan his arms and there were no marks. We had brought his Pandy along – his beloved panda bear that Nanny London had bought some twenty-odd years earlier. He was thrilled as it was always being stolen from his flat or from wherever he was staying. Recently, someone had snatched Pandy back from yet another kidnapping, and had gone to great lengths to ensure that he was reunited with Peter.

Peter was wearing a torn straw hat and said that he was all right, but he didn't look it to me and I fought hard to keep back the tears as this wasn't the place to cry. I had to be strong for his nanny and his sister.

Once inside the venue, it was hard not to enjoy the gig. Pandy and I did step onto the stage, near to the end, as did most of the audience – including his nanny. This wasn't the only time she had seen him perform and she would later go to 'Top of the Pops' at the BBC to see him sing the top-ten single 'For Lovers'. On reflection, a seventy-five-year-old nanny going to a rock 'n' roll gig is quite bizarre, but it's just something she felt she had to do in the hope that she would get the chance to talk to her grandson.

After the gig there was a lot of bonhomie, but our time with Peter was short-lived for we became surrounded by fans of all ages, male and female. I noted there were even some people as old as me – if not older. They were all showering Peter with compliments and attempting to keep him talking. I was keen to get him some water and kept telling people he was very ill. If I said this once then I said it a hundred times. There seemed to be a lot of Japanese girls there and some had even seen him in Japan earlier in the year. I told them that Peter was ill and needed help, but they were oblivious to my protestations and were going wild to get a photo of his nanny, his sister and me. This was most disconcerting for me; how could they shower all this adulation on someone who was, in my mind, so very, very sick? It's even harder to understand what on earth they would want with autographs of his family. An inane idea.

For someone who has never 'adored' a pop star or screen star, it is extremely difficult for me to understand why some people lavish their attention onto another human being who they have never met. For me, it's a strange phenomenon – giving adulation to a person you don't even know.

I admire many famous people, of course I do, but have always been more impressed by unsung heroes: for instance, the mother abandoned by a partner, left alone to bring up a disabled child, or by the patient battling against all odds but who remains cheerful. And there was the family doctor whom I knew as a child who adopted children and gave medicine to the poor and needy. He was, by birthright, a wealthy man but chose to live among the people he served and, after doing his duty in the war, came back to pick up where he had left off to help make the world a better place. These people are my heroes.

I know this is old-fashioned and that we live in the age of instant gratification where success can come all too easily; but, although I have my own views, I do try to understand that, in the world in which we now live, there are a lot of people who just want to be famous or to know someone famous.

Watching my 'sick' child become the focus of adulation from fans provokes, therefore, a range of feelings. On one hand, I want to say 'please leave him alone' because I don't want this adulation to cause him any more harm; it can't be good for anyone in the grip of addiction, with a court case over his head, to be getting the message, 'We love you, therefore your behaviour is okay'. And on the other hand, I suppose I'm always hoping that he may meet with a fan that has come through the same ordeals as him and so could provide a solution.

I think people like Peter for different reasons. As a child, his range of friends was staggering. He was always popular. But standing on the pavement that night, surrounded by fans, he looked so lost and so lonely. It seemed everyone was hanging on his next word. Perhaps it was then that I glimpsed, albeit briefly, the enormity of this responsibility – of people expecting you to be outrageous or wise or wonderful when all you are is another fallible human being.

Just recalling that brief glimpse has triggered another thread that runs through the Peter Problem: the subject of loneliness. Peter often feels lonely and has an acute awareness of this. I have tried to talk to him about it, and listen to him, but the irony is that he is very rarely alone. Perhaps the noise of his fans drowns out the noise of his loneliness.

Once again Peter was gone into the night. He'd been so pleased that we were at The Troubadour gig, which really made the effort worthwhile. Tired, bemused, happy and sad, we three witless wonders – minus Pandy – made our way back across London. In the taxi, on the way, Nanny London said: 'How am I going to tell my sisters Joan and Vera about this tomorrow?'

August brought about a quick descent into serious drug abuse for Peter. This was fuelled by his pending burglary trial, as well as being consumed by guilt from having failed himself, me – everyone. 'Mum,' he would say, 'just forget about me.' I've since learned that this is the norm. Many alcoholics and addicts distance themselves from their families because it's easier for them to cope if they don't think they're hurting anybody else. It would have been easier to forget about him but a mother's heart isn't like that.

Although on the surface he was having a wild time, I'm sure that he was suffering. Only a fellow addict could truly understand this. I have spent almost three years reading everything I could get my hands on – biographies and autobiographies of the many who have gone before, from

Dusty Springfield to The Doors' singer Jim Morrison. On many levels there has been a thread running through that was instantly recognisable – creativity, fragile personality, sensitivity. And some books have helped me a great deal. If I'm honest, in the past I may never have picked these books up – much as I love to read biographies. I had always thought the same old story of a celebrity ruining their life was like an overplayed record. But now they have taken on a new meaning.

In addition, I've read many of the books given to addicts by the authorities, whatever the addiction. It's fairly common for parents, wives, girlfriends and members of an addict's family to take counselling courses of varying types in an attempt to understand. As part of my job as a nurse, luckily, I had already taken some short courses in counselling, listening skills, and those designed to help people change. So I'm fully aware that, until Peter reaches his own, personal rock bottom and wants to change for himself, then there will never be any change. Not for me, not for his son. Until he desires change for *himself* then nothing and no one can help him. I know this. Peter knows this.

Prison. I can scarcely believe any child of mine could end up in prison. Yet prisons are full – overflowing – with people's children. The day my son went to prison is etched upon my memory forever. It's something I've never discussed.

Peter had burgled his band-mate Carl's flat, and I had

bravely travelled over from Holland to attend the court hearing. Peter, his two sisters and I had planned to meet the night before for a family meal in south London. Emily, AmyJo and I waited and waited for him to show until we could wait no more. Sadly, sullenly, solemnly, we went to eat without Peter, but we'd all lost our appetites by this time. We chose a decent restaurant – as close to AmyJo's house as we could, in case Peter turned up – but he didn't show.

The next morning, I felt sick with dread. Shame. Embarrassment. Disgust. Despair. Here was Peter in need – but I also had a sixteen-year-old child, Emily, who I was trying to protect from the sordidness of everything. I couldn't protect Peter now. He had his own fate to face. But I would do what I could for Emily. So, in the end, I decided not to go to court but, instead, to take her back to school for the start of her new term.

Peter's uncle John and his beloved Nanny London went to the court hearing instead. That day – that unforgettable day – was my birthday. My fiftieth birthday. It had always been a family joke that when my fiftieth birthday came along I was going to spend the entire day in bed. Never having ever been in bed past 7.45 a.m. in my entire life, I thought I'd earned the privilege. When the day finally came, the last place I wanted to be was in bed. I didn't know how I was going to get through the day.

I didn't think Peter would turn up to court. Friends had tried to trace him the night before but they couldn't contact him, and we feared he'd do something stupid. And if he did make his court appearance, I couldn't bear the thought of seeing him standing in the dock. I had never thought any child of mine would ever do anything illegal.

I had reached Dover and was just coming out of Tesco when my mobile phone rang. 'He's going to prison,' the voice said. I just thought, 'How on earth can I tell his dad?' But Peter senior already knew – he'd read the news online. Peter was going to prison. I couldn't tell Emily at this point. I couldn't tell anyone else. I didn't believe it myself. I was in complete and utter shock.

I didn't know which way to turn. I dropped Emily off at school and, before we went in, I explained to her what had happened to Peter and that he would be going to prison. I related all the sordid details to her housemistress and asked that she keep an eye on her.

I sat in the car and cried. It was unbelievable. The phone was ringing non-stop. His nanny. His uncle John. Everyone in the family. It had already been broadcast on the news. I switched my phone off and started to make my way home.

When I got back to Holland, the news was everywhere – on the radio, on the television, in the papers. My phone didn't stop ringing: family, friends – they all wanted to know if it was true, how we were coping and where Peter had gone. But I knew that however sick or lost I was feeling, Peter would be feeling a million times worse.

It's difficult to articulate in words exactly how much we suffered as a family at that time. My head was full of emotions ranging from anger, and wanting to give him a piece of my mind, to complete compassion and wishing to hold him and reassure him that everything would be alright. There were also bizarre thoughts, such as being glad my mother wasn't alive to see her grandson in prison; or hoping that neighbours on the military base, or colleagues – even wider family members – wouldn't find out. How could I lift my head up, given all the shame, hurt and embarrassment I was feeling?

As always, and I can't stress this point too strongly, when I begin to think 'Oh, God, how can I get through this?', 'Why me?', or, 'Why us?', I begin to pray. And even when I haven't got the strength to lift my head, something truly wonderful happens in the psyche and immediately I come to the realisation . . . 'Well, why *not* me? Why *not* us?'

I'm not asking for anything in particular, but something takes over and I realise I'm not alone in all this. I was at rock bottom. Things really couldn't get any worse. But I knew I wasn't going to die. And I knew there were people in a far worse position.

And so I had to try to forget personal pain and prepare to deal with the problem in hand – the Peter Problem – even in the vain belief that this would perhaps have given him a short, sharp lesson. You live by the sword, you die by the sword. Life had to continue. But it would never be the same.

Peter went to prison on 8 September 2003 for just over four weeks, though most of the press said he was imprisoned for six months. Hadn't I always blamed the parents for many of the ills of our society? 'No one is at home, any more, rocking the cradle,' I'd often quip, feeling smug that my children had had the benefit of a mother 'at home', always had someone to come home to, always someone there with a sandwich and a smile at the end of the school day.

Hadn't I purposefully ensured that I was there in their adolescent years? Peter, AmyJo and Emily would come in, the tea would be on, and the playing cards would be out on the table for a game of sevens. And didn't I always – by the second round – know who was going out with whom in the sixth form and all the gossip of the day? The children hadn't realised they'd even spoken a word. Likewise, I'd always fought off buying a dishwasher for the simple fact that we rotated the chores: I always washed and AmyJo or Peter always dried. And what had started out as a chore had become a one-to-one session with my kids, several times a week. So much so that when all the dishes were dried, the conversation would carry on because we'd found some level ground on which to talk.

Some say these teenage years are supposed to be a time when mothers can spread their wings a little because the children don't need them as much. But didn't I always know better – that adolescent children need their parents' time more? What a kick in the teeth for someone who curtailed her own career to ensure that she was there to listen and to understand.

How then did it come to this? What had I done wrong? My only son was in prison and it was my fault . . . or so I felt. There is an old Jesuit saying, 'Give me the child at seven and I'll show you the man'. But Peter at seven was as far removed from the man he would become as the East is from the West. These were the thoughts that were running through my head that day:

At seven, Peter was a happy soul, a joy to have in the family, articulate, funny, knew the difference between right and wrong, a mother's dream, an avid reader. *Was at liberty*.

At twenty-four, Peter was a troubled soul, a cause for great concern for the family: inarticulate and fragile, funny, but not the ha-ha type of funny, the line between right and wrong had become blurred, a mother's nightmare, yet remained an avid reader. *Was imprisoned*.

We then had to wait for news of which prison Peter had been taken to and then, much worse, had to wait for word from him. This waiting would become a recurring pattern in the Peter Problem. I'm always waiting, waiting, waiting. Even now. Never knowing what the next day will bring. Always waiting for the prodigal to return.

I can elaborate on this waiting. It's as though your life is on permanent hold. Always waiting for the phone to ring and dreading it when it does. Always waiting for the next day's newspapers and dreading them when they arrive. Always waiting for your neighbour to drop 'Peter' into the conversation. But all I'm ever really waiting to hear is that he's recovered. And still I wait today. The news I dread to hear is that he's dead.

As soon as we were told which prison he was in and had all the details, I wrote one of the hardest letters of my life. What do you write in circumstances like this? I knew it would have to be a letter of unconditional love; a letter assuring him that I didn't judge him. I felt that any criticism would be more damaging; that he would be feeling a million times worse than I was. He was alone in a prison cell with no comfort zone around him. This wasn't a time for chastisement. It was a time to offer support. We didn't know, then, that he would be released in four weeks.

In times of great sorrow, in times of deep despair, it has been a sense of humour that has kept me buoyant. In the past I have nursed Liverpudlians suffering from horrible injuries but their sense of humour has never left them, even in the most tragic of circumstances. And although I left Liverpool over thirty-two years ago, perhaps I've kept a little of that trait. So, in this sorrowful time, in the absolute awfulness of the situation, my pen wanted to write . . . 'Don't drop the soap, son.'

This was September . . . this was prison. What had happened between January and September? A lot had happened. I probably don't know the half of it. But what I do know is more than enough for any mother to bear.

Peter was released from prison early in October 2003. Carl had met him upon his release and there was a well-publicised reunion. The band played together that night at a gig in the Tap 'n' Tin in Chatham, Kent. This was, by all accounts, an amazing gig.

A few days before Christmas 2003, Emily, Peter senior and I travelled from Holland to London to see Peter who had now moved into a small flat. His dad jumped out of the car to have some moments alone with him. Emily and I waited for a few minutes whilst they stood with their arms around each other, and then we joined them. Peter gave me a bunch of flowers as he greeted me, we all cried, and then we took in lots of things we had brought for his flat.

AmyJo joined us later. We knew that Peter wouldn't be home for Christmas this year as he had gigs to perform. AmyJo didn't come home either, she felt that she needed to be in London to be near Peter and to visit Astile and Lisa.

It broke my heart later when we had to leave him.

Chapter 4

The Pen is Mightier than the Sword

Lege et lacrima – Read it and weep

'A lie can make it half way around the world before the truth has time to put its boots on.' *Mark Twain*

THIS WAS A saying that, for all of my growing-up life, I had heard my sagacious grandmother repeat and repeat, never knowing what on earth she meant. Now, sadly, I understand all too well.

Only today, I have read that Peter is twenty-nine, whereas in fact he has just turned twenty-seven. A minor point, yes, but if the media can't be correct in minor, easy-to-check details, how can they be trusted at all? I, like most people, expect to be able to read the truth in black and in white.

It's hard enough having to read the truth written about Peter. It's even harder to read the lies and half truths that are constantly published, not only about Peter but also members of his innocent family who get caught up in the media rush to print anything it can about him – especially if it's controversial. As one young journalist told me, 'He sells newspapers.' But who wants to read about just another troubled young rock musician who's no different from the many that have gone before? The answer is . . . all those with a love of wanting to see a celebrity fall. And Peter is easy pickings. He doesn't retaliate. If he did ever fall, you'd like to think that would be the end of it, but they'd carry on, even then.

Hell will freeze over before I am able to fully understand how a reporter could lie to an elderly grandmother in order to obtain information on the whereabouts of her grandson. But so it was that, in February 2005, a member of the press rang my mother-in-law, out of the blue, in an attempt to loosen her tongue. 'Hello, it's Peter's manager here,' the reporter said. 'I've just come off the phone to Jackie but now she's engaged and I'm supposed to be meeting her and Peter at the rehab, but I don't know which rehab he's in.'

'Oh,' my mother-in-law replied. 'I'm not sure. I'll have to speak to Jackie. Call me back in five minutes.'

When Nanny London called me, I couldn't believe it. 'Peter's manager is sitting in the same room as me,' I told her. Understandably the incident caused untold anxiety to a seventy-four-year-old already struggling to come to terms with the obvious and widely reported problems of her dearly loved grandson. Needless to say, the reporter didn't phone her back.

No matter how devastating it is (and, believe me, it's devastating), it's easier to deal with the truth than blatant lies. These are what cause the most distress – and this is a balance that cannot be redressed unless I step into the public arena. Until now, however, I had no energy for this; I had to keep focused on the problems in hand and keep strong for the problems to come. I feel grossly misrepresented when strangers and family alike tell me what has been written about me – lies such as I have been treated for breast cancer, or I have been standing outside Pentonville prison pleading to get in to see Peter. The list is a long one – almost as long as the inaccuracies. Surely any reporter worth their salt would endeavour to ensure their facts were correct? Why, then, is Peter's child always referred to as Estile (rather than Astile)? I cannot and will not attempt to amend all the misquotes that have appeared. It is a waste of my energy and draws me away from the problem in hand – the Peter Problem.

I know I am not the only parent to suffer as a result of their child's behaviour, nor will I be the last. However, nothing can prepare you for the devastation that is inflicted upon you. The interest from the media is wholly overwhelming and entirely unwanted. Somehow, I can deal with the truth but (and it is a *big* but), when lies and mistruths and inaccuracies are written, I find it intolerable.

Ironically, it is the written word, the very thing that Peter loves the most, which comes back again and again and causes him the most damage. It's doesn't benefit anyone to daydream about how it would be 'If only . . .' I have no idea, in my daydream, what Peter would do for a living but it would have to include the written word. He would make a good critic and would never seek to shatter some aspiring writer's confidence with a stroke of his pen. Rather it would be his way, his pattern, his trademark, to encourage that very person. He has the ability to see the good in people and things.

I'm ashamed to say that, in the past, when I've read some shocking 'news', I may well have been the very first person to say, 'Ah, there's no smoke without fire.' But now, to my utter amazement, I find it hard to believe most of what I read in connection with the lives of so-called 'celebrities' and I find myself empathising with them — knowing that the truth, the whole truth, will have been stretched and stretched from the sublime to the ridiculous, either out of poor reporting or to add shock factor.

It's been an education, of sorts.

Having known Peter for twenty-seven years, it's only through the press that I've discovered things about his early life and about myself that *I* didn't know:

It is written (therefore it must be true) that Peter was Head Choirboy at school. In fact, his school didn't have a choir.

Earlier this year I had come off a particularly hard nursing shift only to read in the paper that Peter had had to be resuscitated on stage the previous night. I called his then manager and was surprised when Peter answered the phone. He never answered this phone:

'Mum?' he said, and I burst out crying. 'What's the matter?'

'Peter, are you alright?' I asked. 'I've just read in one of the papers that you had to be resuscitated last night.'

He laughed out loud and told me to stop reading the tabloids. The story was completely untrue.

A week later my daughters and I went to see Peter and his band, Babyshambles, in Bristol. The following day I read that I had '. . . fled from Devon to be at his bedside as he was in a drug-induced sleep'. The truth was, he was playing a gig and I went up there to watch him.

It is often written that I'm a Catholic although I'm not.

It is written that my husband is an SAS war hero although he isn't. This is a scandalous lie that has caused great distress to the whole family. Had it actually been true, and he had been publicly exposed, what repercussions might that information have had?

The list is long. And my point is simple. Don't believe everything you read in newspapers or magazines. Even photographs can be misleading.

One used to be able to say 'The camera never lies'. But it can. With computers you can do anything.

*

In the final analysis . . . who really cares? Certainly not the reader – nor the headline-hungry reporter. Who cares that yet another musician is ruining his life? But be assured that somewhere there will be a mother, a father, a sister, a grandmother, a wife or a child who cares. Children can also suffer greatly because of their parents' habits. Every single family member does. I have read that for every addict, of whatever addiction, five other people will also suffer. As far as I'm concerned, you could triple that. And they will suffer emotionally, physically and mentally.

Anyone who knows me will know an adage that I hold dear and use with unfailing regularity: 'Nothing costs as much as caring . . . except not caring.' Behind every story of fame and falling are those who, indirectly, have been ravaged by inaccurate hearsay: they've been unable to address the situation – but they have learned to rise above it.

It is during such times that I am helped by faith – by knowing the truth and by leaning on what is right.

Rudyard Kipling's 'If' is a poem I learned as a child and have always loved. Although the whole poem is beautiful, there are just a few lines that mean so much to me in my particular circumstance and have helped throughout the past three extremely long years. Many parts of this poem have become very real to me. I've read or recalled Kipling's words many times and they've brought me considerable comfort. He talks about watching the things you have given your life to being broken, and trying to repair them while being worn down by them. That is exactly how I feel about Peter.

I understand the journalists who write these sensational stories – they are eager young reporters who don't know any different, but they haven't stopped for a moment to consider the pain they're bringing to innocent people. On average, I still get one or two letters a week from the press, and this has been going on for a long time. At least once a week, some member of the press calls – but I don't put the phone down. I'm always polite. I listen to what they have to say. 'As parents, how do you cope with a son who has a drug addiction?' Occasionally it's, 'How do you cope with having a son who is a celebrity with a drug addiction?' They all say they will handle my story sensitively. I thank them for their phone call but make no comment.

I remember one of these phone calls – from a female reporter wanting a story. 'What do you want me to say?' I asked her. 'You twist everything, anyway, and you'll print what you like. There is nothing I can add; there are always lies being written.' I asked her to try to put herself in my position. If it were her brother doing these things, how would she feel? She said she'd been told by her editor that her copy had to be in that Thursday. She then apologised to me and started to cry.

I attempted to write a letter to a journalist – a different journalist – in response to an article she had written in one of the tabloids. This is part of that letter:

Greetings from Dorset.

It is with a saddened and anguished heart that I write this letter. I have nothing against you personally. You are probably a rather nice young lady. I am just another mother who has had the most awful 18 months. And I ask you to think how you would feel if your mother had been exposed like that. In truth, your article was not unkind — just very untrue. I was severely misquoted and the quotes taken out of context. It has caused considerable distress to me and to members of my family. I am a small, private person and am trying to maintain my dignity throughout what's going on around me. I have, to my knowledge, never done anyone any harm — only aspired to serve my fellow man and to treat people as I'd like to be treated. I have worked hard all my life and I do not deserve to be lied about or misquoted. We cannot fight you in a courtroom as we desperately try to protect our anonymity. But I appeal to you as a human being, please consider what you as a hungry journalist are able to inflict on others by the touch of your typewriter.

I didn't send the letter. I would have had to write twenty such letters, and journalists all over Fleet Street would have been saying, 'Have you had a letter from Mrs Doherty?' I felt I wasn't strong enough to fight them. Not then. Probably not now.

You may be wondering, then, if I'm so desperate to protect my anonymity, why I am writing this book. For a start, it's too late for me to protect the anonymity of my family. Time has elapsed. I've grown stronger and now feel that there are other families out there who are going through what I am going through. Perhaps, by telling my story, I can help them in the process.

People often ask me how I cope. And I'll be honest, I cry a lot. A lotta lot! But there is great comfort in tears. It's like a soul washing. It can come on anywhere, uncontrollably. It may be for a minute, it may be for twenty minutes, but it's very therapeutic. I've tried hard to be depressed and I just can't because the tears are like an anti-depressant. I wake in the night and – all mothers and maybe fathers can relate to this – just start crying because I feel Peter is in some danger. I have, as do many mothers, a strong link with all my children and know I have to phone them up the moment this danger-alert happens. They usually say 'Mum, how did you know?' It's part of those apron strings that never get cut – the mystery of being borne of the flesh. A mother can sense when her child is in danger.

I've coined my own personal phrase: 'If at first you don't succeed, cry and cry again.' Tears cover the desire to change things in those moments of awful hopelessness and complete helplessness that parents can feel if something involves their children. In wanting to change things, but not being able to change one iota, the tears fall so easily – but with them comes comfort for a hurting heart.

In the 1946 Walt Disney movie *Song of the South*, Brer Rabbit has a 'laughing place'. I have my 'crying place'. In fact I have several. But one of my favourites is a corner café in the little Dorset town where we live. I can be sure of a good cry there most days – usually after I've scanned the tabloids. I often think about the journalists who write these stories. If only they could walk a mile in my shoes, perhaps they wouldn't be so cruel. But I forgive them because, as I've written, they're young, hungry reporters with no experience of life. They don't care how the families of the people they write about feel, as long as they have a story on their editor's desk. I bear them no evil. I remember another friend, Trish, saying to me, 'You must pray for the reporters.' *Pray for the reporters?* But I know they, too, must be included in my prayers. If only they knew that 'Potty Pete's' mum had been praying for them.

A friend phoned me about six months ago: 'You're not *still* crying are you?' he asked. 'He's not some monster who has murdered someone, he's not a rapist. He's a rock musician and he's doing what a lot of musicians do, and he's doing it to the best of his ability. He's wild and chaotic and he does it well. He's hurting himself but he's not killing anyone!'

Between the sobs I replied, 'He's not *your* son.'

*

Throughout 2005, I remember, everyone was hounding him: the press, of course, but even politicians such as Michael Howard, the then leader of the Conservative Party. He said: 'Here you have a man who takes drugs and gets locked up – yet ends up on the front pages . . . I think many parents will have been rather surprised by the celebrity coverage given to Peter Doherty over the last month.'

I was asked by somebody how this made me feel – that the leader of one of Britain's biggest political parties had mentioned my son in a speech – but I was unable to take it all in at the time. *However*, I was actually in agreement with everything Mr Howard was trying to express. Quite right too. Well done, Mr Howard. I wanted to write to him to tell him that, even as Peter's mother, I agreed with him, but I was fearful of committing anything to paper. These things have a way of being misconstrued – or getting into the wrong letterbox!

In early spring 2006, Peter was held in Pentonville prison on remand for two weeks awaiting a court appearance. I have the letter that he wrote to me from Pentonville and must have read it a thousand times, feeling so low, looking for something – I'm not quite sure what – but trying desperately to read between his words. Despite the circumstances, it is a letter to be treasured.

It has become hard to write back to him because, nowadays, I am so aware that these letters could one day be sold by some unscrupulous person. It has been a source of concern to me that there are letters I have sent to Peter that he has never received. It's such a shame that, as a mother with all of the worries that I have, I am unable to write a true heart-to-heart letter to my son; instead it is guarded, stiff, giving him nothing that might be distorted by another person.

I have always enjoyed writing letters, even as a child. And during the six years I spent as a military nurse, I would often, if there was time, write letters for the injured soldiers to their mums, wives or girlfriends. Mail for the military person is a vital link with home; e-mails and texts are not the same because they lack the flow and the passion of the handwritten word. Back then, there was no modern technology, and so it was a letter or nothing. When writing my Christmas cards, I always endeavour to slip in a hand-written note or letter. More recently, it's just a few words – my letter-writing days are numbered. What does a mother instinctively write about? Her children.

For several years before Peter signed his record deal, letters to friends would read . . . *and Peter is still in London awaiting fame and fortune.*

He now has infamy and much misfortune.

Actually, it was never about the fame or fortune for Peter, it was always about the words, the music – the whole minstrel thing. He is never more content than when singing, either to himself or to a crowd.

Last Christmas, 2005, in most of my Christmas cards I didn't mention any of the children. I just can't bring myself to write about his sisters and not mention him, therefore I skirt around the subject. Being a military family, we have met and made many friends and neighbours over the years and, although we don't keep up with all of them during the year, at Christmas it's wonderful to hear all the news. On average, we give and receive around 130 cards. Most of these well-wishers have their own special memories of Peter and often remind me of how it used to be and what a lovely boy he had been. One lady, Vicki, who had been a neighbour and a friend, reminded me of the time she'd been teasing him over something and Peter had turned the garden hosepipe on her in retaliation. She didn't mind – but *through the kitchen window*!

These days my letter writing is restricted and largely censored even when writing to my daughters. In fact, because of this restriction, because of feeling inhibited, I haven't written to the girls in several weeks now and have to phone and text them instead. But it isn't the same.

I have also longed, over the years, to write and thank the many people who have helped Peter on many levels. There would be so many of these letters, but they remain unwritten.

Peter, nowadays, tries, as best he can, to keep a low profile. It isn't easy for him as he naturally courts attention. He is battling his addictions and feels very weak in that respect. It doesn't help to be labelled constantly as a crackhead or a smackhead. Negative labels bring about negative responses.

As I told his fans back in the early days, Peter is ill and needs all the positive help he can get. Although he says it doesn't bother him, I think it upsets him very much. He is, after all, a very sensitive and vulnerable person. The reporters never ask about his music: the influences, his passions. If the reporter asks him questions he doesn't want to answer, he switches off.

In April 2006, the press carried pictures that caused me great upset – pictures of Peter apparently injecting himself and apparently injecting someone else. Normally when Peter appears in one paper or another, someone will text me the headline and some of the content. Sometimes I'm grateful, sometimes in despair. I never buy these papers, but the regular texts and phonecalls that I receive keep me up to date on what I'm missing. The pictures that day, I was told, were apparently horrifying.

My boss texted to ask if I was okay. 'Yes, I've heard,' I replied. 'Am OK thanks. Am doing a crying marathon – thirty hours so far – can't wait for tomorrow's news; they usually save best till last.' I attempted to leave the house about twenty times that morning. In the end I had to, as we had no milk. I wore a pair of sunglasses to hide my puffy eyes. That very weekend, Peter senior and I had been looking forward to visiting old friends for a sixtieth celebration, all the details had been worked out, room booked, gift ready to go. We never left the house, such was our pain.

Just a few hours before the news broke, at 3 a.m., Peter had called me: he'd been at a gig in Bournemouth and sounded so positive. I told him a joke that I'd heard earlier that day and we laughed. That had been two days on the trot that he'd called and had spoken, both times very positively, about change.

While the world was going mad at what was in the press, Peter was sleeping. Poor sod, he had no idea the trouble he was in. I make no comment on the photographs and believe them to be despicable and beyond words — sickest of the sick, probably. One has to ask the question, is he mad to allow himself to be portrayed in this manner persistently? Does he still trust everyone around him? Is that not crazy? Where the hell will it all end?

Most people would tell me to blame my son, and I say the same thing too, of course I do. Peter is an addict. But there are addicts up and down the country in every town and district and they are not, like Peter, hounded continually by police and press and betrayed by all and sundry.

It is important, now more than ever before, that he keeps out of trouble and attends all his appointments as organised by the courts, and, with all the positive help he is receiving, there is just the slimmest chance that he *will* come through this nightmare.

I have the utmost respect for our police, and have in the past worked alongside them as they strive to keep the peace. I have nothing but praise for them and wholeheartedly apologise to them for the trouble that my son has caused them.

I once attended a policeman in a casualty department who had had his ear bitten off. In an attempt to keep him talking whilst preparing him for theatre I questioned, 'Good Heavens! What animal [meaning the four-legged kind] has done this?'

He replied, 'The drug addict in the next cubicle.'

I am petrified of drugs and the sheer misery, in crime terms, which drug- and drink-related problems bring. Innocent people are being mugged, attacked, stolen from in their own homes, even murdered. Not to mention the crime involved in smuggling, money laundering, prostitution, violence and gun warfare. The list is a long and sorry one.

I support our boys and girls in blue one hundred per cent and know that they have an awful time of it, often caught between a rock and a hard place. They continually have to deal with such terrible events, and have my absolute thanks for their part in fighting the crime on our streets. It would be reassuring to know that every other known addict or dealer was being stopped as often as Peter.

Chapter 5

Time to Move

Carpe Diem – Seize the day

FROM CHRISTMAS 2003 onwards The Libertines were playing gigs but, slowly, Peter's behaviour was threatening to split the band. Although he went to rehab for the second time in May 2004, he didn't stay long – not long enough for me to visit him. I travelled over to London to try and talk to him. As a result of this, and in conjunction with the help of many other people – plus Peter's own desire to 'get clean' – at the end of May 2004 he checked in at his third rehab. I stayed with Peter in London for most of his third attempt.

Peter often says about this rehab that he was blackmailed into it by me – which isn't quite accurate. At the time, I was awaiting – back in Holland – a breast biopsy on a lump that had been found during a routine mammogram. I had put off the biopsy to track him down in London, and I did say that

I wouldn't be going back for the biopsy unless he checked back into rehab — little thinking that would make any difference, but it did! The absolute truth behind this story is that I had prayed, as any mother would, that if my having breast cancer meant that Peter could be saved from his addictions . . . then so be it. I didn't have my biopsy until he was at rehab number four in Thailand.

Being at his side day and night wasn't all bad, either. One of the funniest things that I attempted, out of sheer desperation, was to smuggle Peter's shoes out of his room (there were about twenty pairs in all) in the vain hope that he wouldn't be able to leave easily should he decide to discharge himself. How foolish of me. A nurse pointed out later that, if he really wanted to run away, he probably wouldn't worry about whether he had shoes or not.

It was during this period that I spoke with someone who seemed to know an awful lot about these matters. We met in the foyer of the rehab centre one day. I was crying and I don't recall him telling me his name or why he was there, but he knew who Peter was and that I was his mother and intimated to me that perhaps my son wasn't yet ready to be rehabilitated. I clung to something that he mentioned in passing: he said Peter might find rehabilitation in London difficult and that perhaps Arizona, out in the desert, would be just the place for him. He didn't give the clinic a name, so I have never been sure where he meant, but I locked the thought away. I was soaking up any information I could in my desperation to understand.

During another conversation with a very helpful, erudite individual whom I met briefly in the grounds of the rehab centre, I mentioned that I wanted some way of understanding why anyone would ever take such a drug as heroin (I don't even like to type the word) knowing it was a road to nowhere. He very gently offered an analogy: 'Imagine the greatest orgasm you have ever had and multiply it many, many times.' Again, my Liverpool wit kicked in and, in spite of the seriousness of the conversation, even as the tears streamed down my face, I asked: 'What's an orgasm?'

Having completed his detox at this clinic, Peter didn't go on to the follow-up programme in which patterns of behaviour are challenged or identified. It's now understood that this part of the treatment is absolutely vital and is crucial to real recovery. It isn't enough to have detox alone, but this had to be his decision.

He made his decision.

He was leaving. He apologised, but he was leaving. I understood, but it didn't make me feel any better.

He left me sitting in the clinic surrounded by nineteen pairs of his shoes. I cried and I cried, but I knew that I'd tried my best and I knew that I'd carry on trying.

I remember sitting in the foyer with bags and cases, guitars and books, quite lost and unable to focus on what to do next. Lots of people came to join me. They knew I was Peter's mum. They kissed me. They hugged me. They offered me words of encouragement. They told me this was just one step in his recovery and to not give up hope. These were people who were on their own paths of recovery.

That morning, feeling hopeful, I had written this poem. It had begun as a good day.

'Detox'

This is a good day
Long may it last.
Shoes are returned
Plans have been hatched.

Tremors receding
Cravings are few
Sweating and nausea
Lessening too.

There'll be tears before bedtime
And some in the day
As feelings to run
Fight feelings to stay . . .

But, the cavalry's here
It's mounted its guard
It's stood to attention
The battle'll be hard.

I'll call upon angels
To stand at his bed.

> I'll summon God's spirit
> To reclaim his head.
>
> I'll plead to God's mercy
> For favour and grace
> To bless him with wisdom
> To return him full face.
> *Jackie Doherty, June 2004*

Eventually, I left the clinic and headed for my mother-in-law's. Within a few hours, I heard that Peter was going to Thailand.

Peter and I had heard about a monastery called Thamkrabok, about eighty miles north of Bangkok, which was a drug-treatment centre. Tim Arnold, godson of the actress June Brown (who plays Dot Cotton in 'EastEnders'), told us about it as he had been to the monastery himself. I am very grateful to this young man for his attempts to help Peter.

At that time, everyone connected with my son was overjoyed. He'd made his own decision to go, and we'd heard only good things about the monastery, so I returned to Holland hopeful and happy. We actually knew very little about the monastery and were really relying on hearsay; indeed, to some extent we were clutching at straws – but we felt that this could be the answer to all our prayers. In the back of my mind I acknowledged the fact that he might never return to the West as many recovering addicts are known to stay on and build a new life.

Looking back on this, I realise I knew absolutely nothing about the treatment and what it entailed until I read an article in the paper after Peter had returned. Their detoxification regime made for tough reading but, if this was what it took, then bring it on.

With the Peter Problem, hope is usually very short lived but, that following weekend, I felt at ease, knowing he was safe, out of London, and beginning a journey to normality. At least I could sleep.

The phone rang at approximately 5 a.m. on the Sunday morning. It was Tim Arnold. Peter was leaving the monastery. He hadn't yet been there a week.

This was such hard news to hear. Tim told me there was one English-speaking nun there and suggested that I call her. When I did, she confirmed my worst fears. I begged her not to let him leave the monastery. This wasn't about him heading for London. This was much worse: he was about to be let loose in Thailand – an addict's dream come true. So many things went through my head. I thought, for a start, that Peter would never leave Thailand and I would never see him again.

The nun told me he was a good boy. She told me that she'd looked into his eyes and knew he'd *never* take heroin again. I told her that he was an addict and that his eyes were lying. I begged again, crying, 'Please, I beg you, please. Don't let him leave.'

She wouldn't let me speak to Peter but said she'd give

him a message. I could hear him coughing in the background. No Liverpool wit this time round. 'Tell him mum said to do the *right* thing,' I said. I thought I heard Peter sob and then the phone went dead. I was frantic. Should I go to Thailand? How would I find him? I cried and prayed so hard that morning.

I was feeling so low; so sorry for myself and sorry for my family who were devastated that he'd left rehab number four. Whenever possible, I try to keep close family informed before they hear it on the news or read it in the papers and, at the same time, I make an effort to remain upbeat and positive; they all love Peter very much and are bewildered and heartbroken by his poly-addictions. I was feeling more than sorry for Peter, though – he was stepping into the unknown.

It was Sunday and I went to church. As I arrived, I noticed that my name was down to read the lesson, but felt quite unable to do so. My head was too full of the Peter Problem. I caught sight of the padre and relayed the events of the morning to him. He told me not to go to Thailand and that it was time to 'let go of Peter'. I knew what he meant but, as he spoke, I asked with tears in my eyes and an ache in my heart if that was what Jesus would do. He couldn't answer me. I asked the same question again, searchingly.

Once again I had that feeling of not knowing what to do, or where to go from this point. I felt a new strength and boldly declared that I would read the lesson, after all. It was time to let go and let God.

That was Sunday and it wasn't long before word filtered through that Peter was on his way back home. To this day I still don't know how he left Bangkok. I am amazed that he was able to leave. But his departure from Thailand was down to one person. Through all the mayhem, over these last three long years, this one person has been a constant support and has gone to great lengths to help Peter. I shall be forever grateful but, out of a respect for her privacy, she shall remain nameless.

That Peter had walked out of his rehab was too much for the band to bear. This was now the real beginning of the end of The Libertines.

Whenever I think the Peter Problem can't get any worse, it usually does.

This time, after he'd been back on British soil for only a few hours, he had been stopped by the police for erratic driving and arrested for being in possession of a knife.

It's very difficult to explain what I was feeling.

It was just unbelievable.

Where was it all going to end? How on earth did it all come down to this? A wonderful, happy, bright child – who'd never been in trouble with the police – with a fine future ahead of him. I had no answers then and I still have no answers now.

Back and forth, back and forth between Holland and England. I worked every third night and, in between, would pop back to England. Most of the time it would be a Herculean feat to track Peter down. *Meet me here, meet me there*. I soon knew the London Underground inside out. One summer's day, Peter gave me directions to meet him at a studio. He said the nearest tube station was Old Street, but what he didn't say was that there were multiple exits from the station and each time I exited I got caught in a downpour.

Whenever I'm on a Peter chase, I ensure I have some plasters with me as it usually involves some unplanned walking, particularly if he is with me: his legs are long – he is, at 6 ft 3 in, a foot taller than me – and it's hard to keep up. Just as I'm chasing Peter, the press and his fans are chasing him too. He sometimes runs from the press, but never from his fans. He has a deep respect for his fans. I, on the other hand, have run from fans who are screaming, 'It's Pete's mum!' I can't see what there is to celebrate in that.

And my son is in the grip of a severe poly-addiction. There is nothing to celebrate in that, either.

Life can be very awkward indeed. We want to support Peter as best we can, especially when there is a court case – and there have been many. If I go to court, I often go with Peter's two sisters; we can take comfort and strength from each other and show a united front. But sometimes we don't go in case we are caught in the crossfire of press and fans: then, it can be difficult to maintain any dignity. Sometimes we go incognito, disguised with the help of wigs and other accessories. Sadly, though, on these occasions Peter also doesn't know that we're there.

At the end of that frenzied month of June, I had travelled over from Holland to attend Peter's court hearing for the very serious offence of being found in possession of a knife on the night that he returned from Thailand. AmyJo was working that day but, with great skill and alacrity, Emily and I arrived and entered the courthouse without a sighting of a single camera and sat down to wait for the posting of the lists that would tell us the time and court number of 'our' proceedings. We were delighted that no one was paying us any attention.

As the lists went up, I began to panic. There was no mention of Peter Doherty on any list so I went to speak to someone in charge. Whilst waiting, I rang his manager. Yes, he was due in court that morning. Bow Road Magistrates' Court in East London. We were in Bow Street Magistrates' Court, Covent Garden. We jumped in a taxi and crossed London for the second time that day. The whole place was awash with fans and cameras. There was a man with a mock knife in his head. It was a circus. We walked quietly inside, again unnoticed.

We waited hours.

Peter was ill and didn't turn up.

Emily and I returned to Holland. A wasted journey. We didn't even get to see Peter.

In that summer of 2004, I had been thinking how much easier it would be if my husband and I were in England. The travelling to and fro was both a strain and expensive and I wanted to see more of Peter and my daughters. All three children were in England, the pleasure of a new life in Holland, to which Peter senior and I had been looking forward, had diminished. I thought that if we were in England we could be more of a support for Peter. Looking back, I suppose this was what my husband wanted, too, although we'd never discussed it. It must have been on his mind that this would be a good solution to the problems and he now decided to tackle things head on.

A dear friend of mine was returning from Holland to Dorset – a place I knew and loved – and we'd planned to have a long, lingering champagne breakfast before she left. Because of commitments on both our parts, we could only fit it in three weeks before she was due to leave. We met, we brunched and, as we embraced to say a fond farewell, the last thing I said to her was that I wished we were going to Dorset too.

I hadn't been home more than two minutes when my husband phoned to say: 'How would you like to go to Dorset?'

'When?'

'Three weeks' time.'

He had been posted there. Perhaps I could really help Peter now.

We arrived in Dorset on 6 August 2004 – before my friend.

Being nearer to Peter made no difference, really, except that we could now see our grandson, Astile, more often. The down side of being back in England has been that we quickly became tabloid fodder.

How can you help someone who doesn't really want to be helped; someone who is in denial and who has handed over the controls of his life to class A drugs? I wasn't even sure any more what he was using or how he was using it.

Sometime before Christmas, I was told Peter was going to be interviewed on 'Newsnight' and asked whether the production team could have some video footage I have of Peter performing as a young boy in a band at school (a one-and-only performance). Having checked with Peter if this was all right, I sent the film off with an accompanying letter and soon after the 'Newsnight' team rang to ask if they could read a portion of that letter on air. In the end, they read a portion of the letter but didn't use any of the video footage that I had sent – it was a poor copy as I recall – but on that video Peter displayed a trait that I have seen so often when he performs at gigs. Even at the age of seventeen he was throwing goodies to the audience – then it was KitKats and chocolate bars (all from my pantry) – nowadays it's his clothes, hats, shoes and cigarettes . . . anything. In an odd sort of way that perhaps only a mother would recognise, when he does this I see him throwing away his life; himself.

Only recently, a fan told me of all the things he has that belonged to Peter, some given, some 'acquired', some even purchased on e-bay. When I related this to Peter recently, I joked that I was going to sell his milk teeth on e-bay. He was touched that I still had all his milk teeth and I told him the tooth fairy had sent them to me only for the purpose of safekeeping. If only, as I had done with his teeth, I could wrap him up and keep him safe where he could come to no harm; where no other person could do him any harm; where he could re-learn to enjoy life without the aid of chemicals.

It was quite bizarre to see my son on that particular TV news programme. It felt, suddenly, very personal when 'Newsnight' presenter Kirsty Wark asked Peter how it felt to know there was a very sad woman somewhere, referring to me. He largely avoided the question, but was visibly moved and, in his quick way of thinking, actually turned an immensely deep question into something funny and quite true. He said that if he was a vicar on a bike, I would worry about his bicycle clips being too tight. Which is true! But behind the quips it was plain to see that he was struggling. His fingernails were dirty – a sure sign of something suspect.

It made me laugh and it made me cry. The interview would have had the same effect on me had I not been his mother. Who couldn't have seen in that footage a desperate young man, so keen to appear normal. I thought Kirsty had indeed handled Peter extremely well. She asked many poignant questions and seemed to strike a chord with Peter. It was a good interview. When she told Peter that they had a letter from his mother, he looked to the camera surprised as if to say, 'Oh, no, what now?' Of course, I hadn't 'written' to 'Newsnight'; it had merely been a courtesy note to accompany the footage that I had sent.

Kirsty read out: 'Peter is a gifted poet, writer and thinker. Please be considerate with him, as he is very vulnerable. He is a sensitive soul and has many good points. He has helped so many people. In spite of, perhaps, your first impression of him, he is actually trying to address his problems.'

Kirsty quizzed Peter about his love of poetry and asked him if he could recite any. Peter obliged. Since the programme, many people have asked me for a copy of the poem that he recited on air. There wasn't a title as such but it is referred to as The Bow Poem. This is Peter's original copy:

I knew she wasn't English because she spoke it
    far too well'

I knew she wasn't English because she spoke it
    far too well
    The grammer was goodly,
    The verbs as they should be,
And the slang was bang on the bell

So as the language barrier clanged & banged
    I couldn't hear: hear or see,
    England, London & Bow
    Crumbling into the sea.

No teeth, no hair. But, even at just a few months old, Peter always had a smile.

Another fine mess! Peter aged 20 months and already in training for Glastonbury.

Peter and me on holiday in Venice.

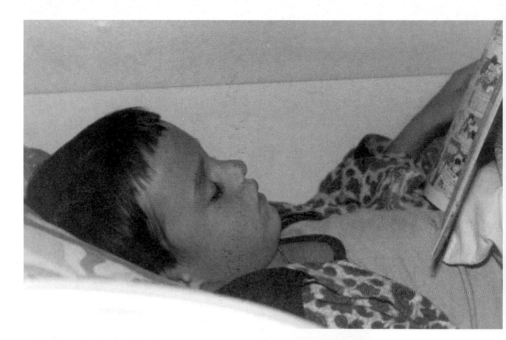

At seven, Peter was a happy soul. Here he is, asleep with his Beano…

…but at 24, Peter was a troubled soul. This picture was taken outside the Troubadour in Earl's Court. His sister Emily was not impressed by all the attention.

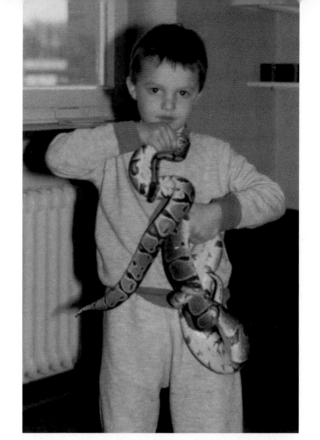

The seven-year-old charmer, playing with snakes in Germany.

Joining the Beavers.

'I'll be back.' Peter visits his first police station in Camden, August 1987.

Peter and me with a baby Emily.

Reaching new heights in Episcopi.

Me, Peter, Emily and AmyJo in Cyprus, 1989.

Neither of us had the hump… Peter and me enjoying a holiday in Cairo.

AmyJo, a squashed Emily, and Peter enjoy another tramps' lunch.

Peter and me at a family wedding in 1990.

Wertach, Germany, August 1991, and another peak climbed by the Doherty family.

'Stone me, what a life!'
Peter indulges his passion
for Tony Hancock.

Peter loved sport and was
good at it, too. Playing
cricket in Blandford, 1992.

He was always such a naturally happy person. This thought is a recurrent one. I awake with it and often try to get off to sleep with it; but, in those times in between, I awake to the nightmare – the new day, the news, the gossip, the pointing fingers – that my only son, my adult child, is an addict.

The idea that I should kidnap him is never far from my mind but I must quickly get rid of those thoughts as they are not helpful at all, not to me, not to anyone, mainly because, although it sounds like the perfect solution, it wouldn't actually work. Where would I take him? Friends tell me to take him to the Scottish Highlands for six months or a year. But such a 'perfect solution' would, in fact, be a very harmful one. If one does intervene when there's a crisis, this can often interrupt and stop patterns of behaviour, but cessation of this can never be maintained until the addict has an earnest desire to change. I am his mother and I feel that it would be a betrayal and that, by kidnapping my son, perhaps I would lose him. It's his life. It's not my life. I can't stop him. I have to accept that I can do nothing except wait and pray.

> He that is down needs fear no fall,
> He that is low, no pride;
> He that is humble ever shall
> Have God to be his guide.
> *John Bunyan*

It is amazing how, in just a few years, one's life can be stood on its head. I have often remarked to people how I had felt as if someone had taken me by the ankles and turned me upside down – such had been the impact on our lives. But I quickly add that, if you can get to the fine old age of fifty with no major problems, then you are also very lucky. Despite all that was happening, therefore, I felt blessed in my trials.

The trials were and are many and, true to life, they are complex. So many problems to keep on top of, twenty-four-seven: the Peter Problem; trying to protect my daughters and letting them see that we will get through this awful time; trying and often failing to be a comfort to my husband; keeping my job going; maintaining any semblance of normal routine. But trials such as these only touch the surface of what we as a family have had to endure.

I always say to Peter when I see him, 'I blame the parents.'

He always replies: 'If you must, then blame them for the good things too.'

But there aren't any good things.

Chapter 6

The Big Issue

Auget Largiendo – He increases by giving liberally

M Y SON, MY prodigal son, is an addict. We say that people take drugs but it's really the other way around: drugs take people. Drugs take everything a person has, from material possessions to their dignity, their hope, and, ultimately, their life. I haven't the answer. I wish that I did.

But I have learnt that, although I can't hide my secret shame (it's there for all the world to see and ridicule and judge me on), and although I have suffered indignities that cannot be imagined, I feel that, in my pain, I have been able to help other people in a way that I never thought possible. As a result of the whole world knowing my son as Britain's worst drug addict, I cannot hide.

There are, however, many people out there who are able to hide but who yearn to talk about it. And because my son is the worst example, people feel safe with me and open their hearts to me about their own children and their problems and, more often than not, about the 'secret' problems that they, themselves, are struggling with.

As a young man, Peter would always purchase the *Big Issue*, often using his last pound to do so. Since the Peter Problem began, I had felt drawn to do the same and, whenever I was in England, I'd stop and buy a copy in the hope I could speak to the seller. My experience, limited as it was, led me to believe that many of the *Big Issue* sellers had battled, or were battling, some of the problems that Peter was facing.

'Are you far from home?' I'd usually ask. These days, I say: 'I have a child like you. Just tell your mum that you are safe, even if you don't want to tell her where you are.'

The many stories that I have heard are very varied and all are desperately moving, but nothing can prepare you for hearing that they have nobody at all to call, or that they feel their mother wouldn't care where they were.

One Christmas, a particularly cheery young vendor shouted cheekily across the pavement: 'Now madam, you'd like to buy a *Big Issue* wouldn't you?' He was so positive. He looked so happy and gave the impression that he had so much to look forward to. He had no idea that, despite my outward appearance, my world was in turmoil. Here was a grey-haired old biddy who looked as though she hadn't a care in the world. Nothing could have been further from the truth.

As we engaged in light conversation, the money paid, the

copy in hand, I remarked upon his 'joie de vivre' and a moving conversation ensued. He told me a little of his life. He wasn't yet 'home and dry', probably never would be; but (with help) he had finally, after many years, addressed the complex problems that had brought him to the streets. He was learning a trade and, for the first time in a decade, was going home for Christmas.

I told him that I had a child similar to him, but didn't expound and let him talk. After telling me his story, he asked whether my child had ever beaten me to get money. Had my prized meagre possessions ever been stolen to fund a consuming habit?

'No,' I said.

To date, I have never experienced anything like that but, having spoken to so many people for whom this is a regular occurrence, my heart goes out to them.

My earliest memory of anything to do with drugs or addicts was when I was a young child. I was staying at my nan's house and it was a Sunday teatime. We were watching television and the actor David Kossoff appeared as a host on a popular television programme – I believe it was a religious programme. My nan had said how sorry she felt for him. She told me his son was a drug addict who had died aged twenty-five from a drug-induced heart attack. I had never heard the expression 'drug addict' before and asked her what it was. Even at that age it appalled me.

Isn't it always the case that when you hear something

you've never heard before that you often hear it again relatively quickly? So it was in this case: no sooner had I heard the phrase 'drug addict' than I found out about the talented Ray Charles who battled heroin addiction for two decades.

I quickly learned that many famous people had a problem with alcohol or drugs or both. Marilyn Monroe. Billie Holliday – another fallen prey to heroin. If these people had everything, I wondered – young and naïve as I was – how could they be so unhappy? During my early twenties, I had travelled home on leave from the army (this seems a strange turn of phrase but it simply means that I had a few days off duty and had gone home to see family and friends). I noticed that a film of Holliday's life story – *Lady Sings the Blues*, starring Diana Ross – was being shown in Liverpool. However, none of my friends was free to go to the pictures. A Dilemma. Going to the pictures alone was not a cool thing – at least not then. However, I really wanted to see this film so I had no choice. All by myself, I sat and wept until the closing credits; it had really upset me. I was just out of my teenage years – and from a city – so of course I 'knew about drugs', but the reality was that I really didn't know a thing about drugs. This film moved me.

None of my friends ever took drugs. It wasn't part of our vocabulary.

In the sixth form, I was invited to go to a party with a friend's brother. He was a student at the art college in Liverpool and I was thrilled. We went to The Cavern Club first and then on to the party. I remember being so excited, these people seemed so cool (or 'with it' as we used to say), but I had been there only about ten minutes before I knew that something wasn't right. I hadn't been offered or seen anything, but my instinct was to leave.

I left alone. I called my dad from a phone box but had no idea where I was. He told me to read the address panel and not to move until he arrived – he knew the area as he was a Liverpool cabbie. I had never realised there was another side to the city. This was a student zone. This was a pseudo-hippy zone. That was my only personal experience, as a teenager, of anything suspect. I had no proof that anything was even going on. It was pure conjecture; but, if that was 'with it', I would rather be without it.

Over the years, there have been so many names, famous or otherwise, connected with drugs or alcohol that it makes for harrowing reading. Some years ago, we were stationed in Germany and I was in the library on camp when I spotted several Danielle Steele books – big thick books – and recalled that I had heard her speaking on the radio about the book she had had to write. It was called *His Bright Light* and she had done it for her son, Nick Traina. Nick was a punk-rock musician and a manic-depressive who became involved in drugs and killed himself at the tender age of nineteen. In all her years of writing, this book had been the most painful, and she recalled, in her talk, how hard it had been to document her troubles.

I couldn't find it on the library shelves and ordered it

through the librarian. I still don't know what drew me to the book because at this time there was no Peter Problem. Perhaps it was because it was another mother's tale, not a work of fiction. Some time later, it arrived and it was a very moving, very graphic account of how she had coped with an addict child. He, too, was a talented musician, although as a child there had been some troubled moments. What I remember most from the book was that, when her son was in an emergency room after overdosing on some substance, a so-called friend had come in and given him some drugs.

These days I read anything to do with addiction, I have a Narcotics Anonymous handbook and I read biographies and autobiographies of anyone from Janis Joplin and Jimi Hendrix to Brian Jones and Kurt Cobain. Sadly, the list is a long one.

There are well-meaning people who campaign against many injustices. There are many anti-war demonstrators, for instance, but where are the protestors against the war in our streets and in our society? This is the drug war that is invading our youth and causing havoc in our neighbour-hoods – but this is a silent ravaging war that penetrates the very fabric of life, destroying lives, destroying families and destroying communities.

Drugs are everywhere, now, and in every strata of life, from school children to politicians. As a parent, I strove to ensure my children knew of the dangers of drugs and all their related issues – and these are *big* issues. They'd all received the relevant information from home, school and family, and been blessed with a healthy, well-balanced sense of self-esteem. How could any child of mine embark upon a path of drug taking when he knew all the facts? Of course, it is the same with smoking cigarettes. An analogy of this is best expressed in the following:

A man enters a local shop.

'Have you got any Soya sauce mate?' he asks.

'Sorry it's off the shelves,' the shopkeeper says. 'It's got *that* ingredient in it.'

'Oh! I'll take some Worcester sauce then pal.'

'Sorry, it's off the shelves, cancer scare.'

'Spicy chicken wings?'

'Off the shelves too.'

'Cottage pie?'

'No, sorry.'

'Hamburger relish?'

'All off due to a scare.'

'That's maddening, pass me a packet of cigarettes then please.'

'No, problem! That'll be £4.52.'

The point is that, in spite of all the dangers and warnings, people *will* seek out and experiment with illegal substances even when the risks are known. This is an enigma to me. I find it so hard to understand this side of human nature. Common sense tells us that no one sets out to become an alcoholic or drug addict.

In an attempt to understand or make sense of what we call 'dabbling with drugs', we pigeonhole people and stereotype them. It's fairly well established that victims of abuse of any kind can commonly develop a drug or alcohol problem (often a combination); some youngsters are curious and experiment with anything available and we're well aware of the lonely person who likes a tipple or two.

I suppose if you ask a heroin user why they take drugs they'd say it's because they like it; but underneath lie a multitude of other reasons. Why does my son take drugs? Honestly, I don't know. I don't know if I'll ever know.

You may be reading this thinking 'Not me!' But I believe that, given the circumstances, it is possible that it could happen to any one of us.

At this juncture, I feel very strongly that now is the right time for me to express my total abhorrence of drug taking. I do not condone any use of drugs whatsoever other than those used by sick people for an illness. Nor do I condone any illegal activity and believe that the laws that we have are for the good of society as a whole and should be adhered to by everyone.

Whilst I detest the hedonistic ways my own son has been caught up in, I am able to differentiate in my feelings towards the whole situation. I hate the sin, but love the sinner. My love for my child is no less than it ever was, but that doesn't mean to say that I condone his behaviour in any way.

Many people love in different ways and some parents eventually find they have to move to an area of 'tough love'. This means many things and in varying degrees. It could mean for a parent or loved one simply to have nothing to do with the wayward person; to draw a clear parameter, a fixed constraint or boundary. Each parent copes in his or her own way. Sadly, some people have very little love in their lives and it is no surprise that they, in return, find it hard to show love. Those of us who are loved or feel love are able to share it.

'You can give without loving, but you can't love without giving.'

And so it is that I have moved on, emotionally speaking, in my relationship with *Big Issue* sellers. These days, it's a privilege to buy a copy, to help with the issue of home-lessness and any other problems associated with it. It's something that can happen so easily to any one of us or to a member of our family.

The bigger issue here is addressing the problems that younger children now face every day – probably more often than we care to believe. We knew where Peter was as a young person. He never roamed the streets as a child, was never left to his own devices. He chose this path much later, as a man. But what about the children who do roam the streets unaware of what dangers there are?

I remember talking recently with a mother who was having difficulty controlling a child of fourteen. Her daughter wanted to stay out till all hours – like her friends

– and had actually defied her mum and stayed out at a party all night one school night. The mother was heartbroken and, worse still, had no way of stopping her daughter. This situation is now very common.

When talking with *Big Issue* sellers, I usually ask them how old they were when they had their first alcoholic drink. Then I ask how old they were when they first used drugs. The answer they mostly give is not an answer that I like to hear. It is not unsual for twelve- or thirteen-year-olds to experiment with drugs. I have even heard of even younger children than this, but twelve or thirteen is common. Once a child is 'in' with a set of friends, it's difficult for them to escape, even if they want to, and so patterns begin to emerge. Drug dealers are always on the lookout for new customers and pretty soon the 'smart' kid realises that he or she could easily support their habit by just selling the drugs themselves. This then takes them to a different level. Horrifying isn't it? These are the real big issues that we face now as a society.

Before the Peter Problem, I knew of few parents whose children were addicts: it was mainly the children of celebrities who would hit the headlines, not people that I knew personally. But since the publicity surrounding my own son, people have made their problems known to me – with, I may add, some relief to themselves. They have opened their hearts to tell me all that they have had to endure.

It has been a journey for me to enter into a world that

bears no resemblance to my own because, in their stories, they have been beaten, they've had money stolen from them, had items go missing from the house, seen their child come home regularly under the influence of drugs, and much worse. Talking with other parents has also helped me to know that the person to whom I am talking can truly understand my pain without my ever having to mention it.

There's also a real sense of wonderment in listening to how other people cope. Some people don't cope very well at all and hit the bottle themselves, or their marriage splits apart, or financial stresses set in. The troubles of many parents are as heartbreaking as the addicts' stories. A point that I also find quite upsetting is when I'm told that they have more than one child who is an addict. This is an all-too-common tale. Can you imagine that? It is just the most awful thing.

Perhaps we need to be looking at and listening to the children themselves, asking them what it is – or what isn't – in their lives that makes them want to even try drugs. I'm clutching at straws as I struggle for an explanation other than that they just want to fit in with their peers, or that they want to be 'grown up', or that they are, in some cases, trying to blot out some kind of pain. Whichever way, before they know where they are they are hooked.

It would be far too easy to oversimplify the reasons why a young person takes drugs or drinks. These are very complex issues – and it isn't right that we stereotype drug users. But the common denominator is that there are drugs readily available on virtually every street corner. They're there in ample supply, as is borne out by the steady dropping of prices.

If you have young children in the family, listen to them: ask them questions about themselves, about their peers and their views on life.

Children are precious – not just to their parents, but precious to society as a whole.

Chapter 7

For Pete's Sake

Quid nunc – What now?

SO OFTEN, THESE days, children attend nursery at such an early age, through parental choice or parental need, but I was very fortunate in that I was able to spend those early years with the children. We didn't have any spare money but there was plenty of love and time.

Peter was a very healthy boy when he was growing up and, apart from croup as a baby (which would be easily sorted by a steamy bathroom and some Vick's rubbed on his chest), together with the odd earache and the usual childhood diseases, there was nothing else really wrong. He once had a nasty bout of mouth ulcers when he was about eleven and, later, Osgood-Schlatters disease which sounds bad but is a very common complaint amongst youngsters. It affects the knees and is usually literally 'grown out of'.

He also suffered from hay fever and, when he was

seventeen, he had a nasty experience on his way to an exam. We were living in the Midlands, just on the outskirts of Nuneaton, and he was cycling to school from Bramcote to Bedworth. I later got a call from the school asking if I could pick him up as his hay fever was making him most unwell. I had never known him to have hay fever and was a little shocked and a bit put out because I had a lot to do. When I saw him, his face and his eyes were horribly swollen but he told me they were better than they had been. That morning, he had taken the back roads into school and ridden his bike through fields of rapeseed. He was in a terrible state. As a nurse, I see a lot of hay-fever sufferers and have never seen such a severe reaction as this.

I suppose it was because of his general good health that he hardly ever missed a day at school. His father and I have been reading through his school reports recently, to remind ourselves of the person he used to be. We were amazed at his punctuality record and his excellent level of attendance. During the three years he was at one school, he never had one day off. I think he always liked school.

As a school child, Peter was always bringing people home. He had so many friends, often of different cultures and faiths: Japanese, Indian, French, German and Russian. For a period he attended Dalton Middle School in Dusseldorf, Germany, where local residents would pay privately for their child to attend the local military school as it was English speaking. It is often written that Peter was a Public School boy; in fact, nothing could be further from the truth.

When he was about three-and-a-half, Peter went to an English-speaking kindergarten on the army base in Germany. I can remember being a little taken aback when the supervisor commented on what a clever boy he was — he knew all his colours, he could count and understood the maths involved and was actually reading by then, too. He knew his alphabet and always, always had a smile on his face and a twinkle in his eye. She also marvelled at his concern for others. He was a happy child.

When Peter started at 'proper' school, aged five, he caused a disturbance during the first week by stopping the proceedings of the weekly assembly because he thought the headmaster had made a mistake. The head had been awarding points to various children and called out various names, one of which was Amy. Peter stood up, suddenly, and informed him that it wasn't Amy that he was giving the points to. It caused a stir, and eventually Peter was consoled and it was explained to him that the points weren't for AmyJo but for another child called Amy.

At school in Cyprus, he caused a furore when he 'confessed' to something that he didn't do. As I recall, someone had broken or misplaced a pair of scissors. The teacher knew who had done it but, in an attempt to flush him out, told the entire class that some restriction would prevail until the culprit owned up. It was too much for Peter to bear. Innocent though he was, he owned up thinking that he would be helping the whole class. Instead, he got a jolly good telling off at school and then another from his dad after he came home. This was Peter.

In Cyprus, he loved it when school was out for the day. Over there, school began much earlier than in England and the children finished at lunchtime because of the heat. There was very little television, apart from which he was far too busy to watch it anyway. He would head straight out after lunch and, quite apart from the days when we went to the beach, there was so much to do. There was a swimming pool on the base, and Peter was always a competent and able swimmer, but it was the 'Bondou' that he adored. The Bondou was the name used for the wastelands that surrounded the army camp. It was a wonderful place for a young boy to play in, but it wasn't free of dangers – there were snakes and biting insects and all manner of lizards and creepy crawlies, and feral cats roamed freely in abundance. Peter would play there with his pals for hours on end. It was truly a boys' paradise: paw paw trees, cacti – a rough and uncultured terrain.

One day he came running home – or, rather, walking quickly in a very suspicious manner. 'Mum, mum, look at me!' Dear God, what was a mother to do? There he stood before me on our back porch with a huge snake around his neck. He was absolutely chuffed. Meanwhile, I was frozen on the spot, about to collapse in sheer and utter disbelief, but Peter had it under control, removed it, and took it safely back onto the Bondou – once he was sure that I had seen his snake-charming talents. Only later did I find out that it was a poisonous snake.

All the boys were the same. There would be buckets of this and buckets of that, collections of frogs, lizards, geckos, chit chats – he still bears the scar on his lip where a lizard was once hanging from it. He thought it was great fun to have them all over his face. Wherever Peter was, there would be a lizard of some sort not very far away. He loved to read about them, and we would all get the anatomy and physiology of each specimen. You just never knew what you'd find in his pockets and I took great care to turn them out rather than putting an unsuspecting hand inside. It was dangerous work, indeed, and not for the faint hearted. To find a dead cockroach is not a mother's delight; however, it was a good thing when they were dead because the live ones were much more frightening.

The older children took part in all kinds of activities – there was always something going on. For instance, Peter and AmyJo inevitably had the lead parts in school plays. As a family, we explored the island from one end to another – all the beaches, the Troodos mountains, skiing in the morning, beach in the afternoon, the markets of Famagusta (when we were able to get a pass to visit the other side of the island), Nicosia, St Hilarion, Bellapais (famous for the Tree of Idleness, immortalised by the author Lawrence Durrell in his book *Bitter Lemons*), Kyrenia and many historical ruins. There was just so much to see and enjoy as a family and, of course, the pleasure of eating out together. It was a delight to be able to afford to take three children out to eat at least once or twice a week. The whole event would last for hours and often we would be in a local orange grove eating amid hanging oranges. Peter and Emily would catch frogs while we waited for our food to arrive. Peter has fond memories of Cyprus and made many friends during our time there.

He was an interested and interesting child with a well-developed sense of humour; it was always a delight to have him in your company. He was gifted at mimicking people. He used to impersonate Margaret Thatcher and have us all in stitches, not just for the almost-perfect pitch but also for the content of his little act. He had a special skit worked out for poor old granddad, which consisted of Mrs Thatcher ridiculing taxi drivers – in particular, Percy of Liverpool. It was hilarious. His grandparents were so disappointed when he no longer 'did' the voice, but he always had something else up his sleeve.

Peter also listened to the radio from a very young age. He would ring in to some programmes pretending to be someone he wasn't and cause a stir. Some mornings before school, he would hang around the phone waiting for a call back from the local radio station. 'Who are you this morning?' I would ask.

He and his dad tuned in to 'phone-in' football programmes in the car on the way back from a match, the callers to which were usually disgruntled football fans. The two Peters would laugh out loud together at some of the 'grumbles' on air. 'I think that's the chap who rang in last week,' Peter would tell his dad.

Much has been written – inaccurately – about Peter having once been a choirboy and, in one report, he had even been exalted to Head Choirboy at his school. Perhaps Peter himself promoted this image; he often does that in a satirical manner when dealing with some ridiculous question. I read recently that he'd been asked when he had last attended confession. I howled. To my knowledge he's never been to confession in his life. I wish he had! It wouldn't do any harm.

The photo of him dressed in a cassock, looking angelic (which the papers keep printing), came about in the mid-eighties. We were in Germany, and Peter would have been about seven or eight. One Sunday, AmyJo, Peter and I (Emily hadn't arrived at this point) were sitting in church when the padre put out a plea for more people to join the choir, as most of the choir's members, being military personnel and their families, had been posted. The stalls, therefore, looked bare. As the padre announced the next hymn, Peter got up from his seat and walked down towards the front of the church. The padre was stunned. 'Where are you going Peter?' he asked, puzzled, as Sunday school hadn't started. Little Peter, who was only six-and-a-half at that time, pointed to the choir stalls and said, 'I'll sit there, I'll sing in the choir,' and on he continued. He sat himself down. It was such a funny moment but we all remained poker-faced until he'd gone out to Sunday school, and then the padre informed us he had never had such a quick and positive response to joining the choir.

It was a rare moment. No one could have planned for that. And, as if it wasn't hard enough to juggle the timetables for football, cubs, brownies and other important activities, now Peter decided that he had to attend choir practice each week. I think that he attended all of seven practices before our family, too, was posted – this time to Northern Ireland. However, after the service one Sunday morning, and before we left, I took a photo of him in his cassock, never knowing that this would one day be in the national press.

It would be some years later that Peter and his elder sister decided that they would like to be confirmed. Their dad was overseas in the Middle East and we were back again in Krefeld, West Germany. We were there when the Berlin wall came down in 1989. In fact, we have had three postings to this wonderful part of Germany.

Although I have a deep faith, I have never forced any of the children to attend church. There is no point in that at all; of course, I have prayed that they would know for themselves the joy in having a faith but I've left them to make their own decision.

I was very pleased for AmyJo and Peter and hadn't expected it at all. Very few of their close friends went to church. I understood how hard it must have been for them both, as young people, to feel different from their peers, especially as their mum was also a Sunday-school teacher. It just wasn't cool.

The day of their confirmation arrived and we had to travel for over an hour to another church where the Bishop to the Forces would be visiting. That morning, I had prayed that this would be a real experience for each of them and that they could find a relevance in the service and recognise the importance of what they were about to profess.

They were smart kids and they could see that, in our family, I was the only person who was bothered about going to church. They had often heard me jokingly scoffed at by their uncle Arthur, my brother, who would tease me about 'this faith'. It still happens today. 'There's no such thing, Wackie,' he'd say, using his nickname for me. These days, he is gentler with me; I believe even he can see that it is only my faith that sustains me. I knew that, for the kids, it would be only a matter of time before they, too, would stop going to church as other pressures began to pull their attention away.

The service was very relevant for Peter because the sermon was about 'football' — what a wise Bishop: he had caught their imagination and wrapped it up in something that would appeal and was topical.

By comparison, when Emily, his younger sister, was being prepped for confirmation at her school, she wrote me a most beautiful and moving letter explaining her feelings, asking that she be excused from taking confirmation. She felt it would be hypocritical and that it was something that she most definitely didn't want to do. It was a letter that any Christian parent wouldn't really want to read but it is a letter that I treasure very much and, when I called her that evening, I said how proud I was of her and that of course she must follow her heart. She never got confirmed.

The mind plays funny tricks on a mother. In times of despair, mine often wanders back to the times I have spent with Peter that I most cherish. One such occasion was when he and I went on a trip to Egypt in 1988. We were living in Cyprus at the time and short trips from Limassol to Israel and Egypt were affordable. Package tours were not my husband's cup of tea and so, when it was convenient, I took AmyJo to Israel. Some weeks later, Peter and I set off for Egypt on a three-day cruise. As soon as we boarded the vessel, Peter was off. 'Can I go and explore, mum?'

Knowing he was safe on board – and a fundamentally sensible child – and after issuing him with the usual warnings, off he went. I expected him to return in a few minutes, but he had been gone almost an hour when I began to worry. The cabin was tiny with just enough room to breathe, but I couldn't leave it in case I missed Peter.

Eventually he turned up with a huge smile on his face. 'I'm in the table-tennis competition,' he said. 'I've won my round and am through to the next one.' He was completely oblivious to time or the worry he had caused me. This set the theme for the trip. On the day we were to visit the Pyramids, the coach stopped and the courier announced that we were either to walk the rest of the way or to take a horse and cart or a camel. I was hoping that Peter didn't want to take a camel – I didn't much fancy it myself – but of course he did, and that's how we made rest of the journey. It cost us a pound sterling to get on the camel but five pounds to get *off*!'

'Would you like me to take picture?' the camel driver asked, hopefully.

'What a nice man,' I thought. Silly woman – it was going to cost me another fiver to have that photo taken. Then I noticed that Peter's camel driver was taking him off at full speed in another direction. I was panic-stricken, but soon caught on – another five pounds. Of course I didn't pay up for Peter or the camera to be returned . . . once bitten and all that.

That holiday wasn't all fun, either. It was August and unbearably hot. We were used to the warm weather, as we had been living in Cyprus for over a year. However, as tourists, it was difficult, especially queuing to enter a pyramid at Cairo. We were grateful to have a small respite from the glaring sun, only to find that, as you enter the pyramid, it's like being a sardine squashed between oily, sweating people. And if that isn't enough, you then have to climb down the pyramid steps in the most unusual manner. The steps have a piece of wood across them, which ensures that as you climb down the steep and dark steps, your feet are turned upwards. Peter and I laughed, both thinking the same thing and singing the song 'Walk like an Egyptian'. If Peter reads this, he'd definitely add his own memory from Egypt: of getting a clip around the ear beside the Sphinx when he persisted in walking ahead of me and not keeping within eyeshot. He didn't need telling again.

Needless to say, back on board the ship, he won the table-tennis competition.

From an early age, Peter didn't need a lot of sleep and used to read late into the night. As a small child, he devoured books at an alarming rate and understood their content, too. It's this Peter that I like to think about at the moment. As did most young boys, he loved the *Beano* and *Dandy* comics. He once used a smart word during a conversation and, when he was asked how he knew the word and its meaning, he said he'd read it in the *Beano*.

At night, before Peter senior and I went to bed, we'd check on the kids and would often have to remove a book from a sleeping Peter's hands. He had many favourites – one in particular was a thick boys' book full of general knowledge. From the age of about seven, he knew all his capital cities and all the flags of different countries.

Once, when he was a young lad, I found him reading a copy of Brecht. I had to look up who Brecht was and discovered he was a German playwright who was awarded the Stalin Peace Prize in 1954. I have always been so proud of Peter's reading abilities, not being the brightest button myself. Even today, his apartment is crammed with reading material. When he decided to leave university, I remember him saying to me, 'Mum, I will never stop reading . . .' He was closing the door on that part of his life, but reading is something he loves. He is as driven to read as he is to write. And this has never changed.

His ability to learn and retain knowledge never ceased to amaze me. I remember one year during the December before his fourth birthday when we were walking through a mall in the south of England where piped music was being played. I hadn't even been aware of any background music – I was oblivious to anything but the shops as I had lots of Christmas presents to buy. As we were walking, Peter stopped and declared loudly to all and sundry: 'Mummy, this is Tchaikovsky, listen, listen.' He was right – it was *Swan Lake*. People started asking me how old he was in utter amazement. Here was just a dot of a child wildly excited by the fact that a piece of music he knew was being played over the air. I explained that it was from a cartoon that he loved.

Peter was such a talented child; from his first spoken poem to debates at school – he had such a way with words. When he was in the sixth form, he was at one time part of a debating group and entered a school competition with a cash prize for the winning team. Peter was discussing his topic with me beforehand and I said, 'Listen son, that topic has been done to death – why don't you pick another theme?' But he believed in what he was doing. Peter had been very affected by the whole Hillsborough incident and had read all he could about it in the press. He had asked Nanny Liverpool to go to the Anfield Stadium and say a prayer for the victims of the Hillsborough Disaster.

On the night of the competition, local dignitaries turned up to judge as I sat comfortably to await the turn of Peter's team. He spoke with great passion on the Hillsborough Disaster and, during his summing up, I could hear some people crying in the auditorium. His team won.

At one of the schools he attended, Helen Sharman, the British astronaut and scientist, came to visit; she was working on a BBC production about the Blandford Fly – a flying insect peculiar to that part of the world and which flourished on the River Stour. Over the years it has brought much misery and suffering to anyone it has bitten, and Helen was visiting Peter's school to talk to the children about it. Peter hadn't been at the school very long and knew nothing about the Blandford Fly. But who did the BBC choose to interview? Peter.

When the programme was aired, we watched Peter's hand move across his face as he spoke to the interviewer and all I could see (as a mother) were his dirty fingernails.

Over the years Peter has had many visits to the BBC. In the mid-nineties, he and I applied to be contestants on 'The Generation Game' and travelled to London for the selection process. Peter was truly amazing at improvisation and we were successful. However, the date of the shoot landed right in the middle of the week we'd booked for our holiday: Peter was off to stay with an old school friend at his Mediterranean home and the rest of us were visiting France to revisit some of the graves from World War I before heading for a short break at Euro Disney.

While we were away, I called Peter one night – he was then sixteen – to see how he was. He told me that had been on a boat and really was having a good holiday before saying, 'Mum, we're in the middle of dinner. Guess who I am sat next to?' I had no idea. 'The President,' he said. He wasn't lying either. Here was my son having dinner with the President of a Mediterranean country and all I could say was: 'Well, I hope your nails are clean!'

I was once very concerned that Peter had to move school right in the middle of his GCSEs. Always the scholar, he was almost a year into his studies and was taking thirteen subjects when the awful news came that the entire regiment would be moving to a new location. We then found out that the new school would only allow him to take eleven subjects, Peter handled it with his usual aplomb. A few teachers from the school he was leaving really didn't want him to go, and one of them even offered him a home until he had finished his exams.

Despite having to change schools at such a crucial time, he had glowing reports in almost every subject. He and AmyJo moved from a small Dorset town school to Nicholas Chamberlaine School – the largest in the Midlands – where he sat his GCSEs and A-levels. In the few years that they were there, AmyJo and Peter excelled – as did many other children. The teachers were truly dedicated and I have only thanks and admiration for them. They really cared and it showed.

Around this time he started his own football fanzine, which he called 'All Quiet On The Western Avenue'. Queens Park Rangers football club was the love of Peter's life and still is. He and his dad would go to a match whenever they could, sometimes with his cousins Ben and Adam and their father Liam, Peter senior's brother-in-law. All of them are huge QPR fans.

A fanzine is, of course, a fan magazine – and Peter's was extremely successful. He was very particular about the artwork and soon letters began arriving for him daily from all over the UK; even the odd letter from abroad, all of them offering contributions or remarking on what a good magazine it was. Before long Peter was invited into the Director's Box one Saturday at Loftus Road, where QPR are based. His dad borrowed a blazer from the Adjutant of the Regiment for the occasion. An adjutant is usually a young officer who works directly for the commanding officer and our Adj at the time was about the same build as Peter – who was now growing and growing. For all those years, Peter had had suits or blazers and now – just when he really needed one – he didn't have one that fitted.

Peter *played* football too; wherever we were he always joined the local boys' football club in the hope of getting in the team. Even in Germany he joined the local German boys club, which improved his German vocabulary nicely. If his dad was away, I would take him to training. One night we cycled there – it was only a few kilometres from where we lived and was a lovely summer's evening. After training, I cycled back to collect him but we could see each other across the fields and both of us decided to hide. We had both had the idea to surprise the other but, after a long time, each waiting for the other one to appear – the joke gone wrong – we headed home.

Peter's passion was football. Even now he makes me squirm when he says that all he ever wanted was a decent pair of football boots. I never bought the most expensive because I had three children to buy shoes for. Perhaps that's why he has so many shoes today.

Often, as a young man, he could be seen sitting alongside someone, just listening. He is a great listener and could teach many people about the art of listening. His grandad once said to me: 'Our Peter is so wonderful to talk to.' I had to laugh to myself because, as I recall, Peter had hardly said a word at all – but he had made my dad feel that they'd had a good conversation. Even these days, for all the reports that he's glassy-eyed and distracted, he really listens and is always astounding me when, at some later time, he feeds back to me what I have previously told him. Woe betide me if I try to change one iota of my previous conversation. He'll remember.

It's well documented that he likes to talk to the ordinary man, to the down-and-outs, to listen to their stories. At one family event, some years ago, Peter was chatting to a Lithuanian man who had been through a lot of upset and had endured many trials in his life. He had left his home and family as a young soldier many years before and told Peter of all the things he loved and missed from his home. This man had a captive audience and one who was keen to listen to his struggles, and he thanked me for having such a polite boy. He couldn't remember when he had last been able to talk about home. Peter told me later that evening on the way home that he would like to get a concertina and learn to play it; it was one of the things the family friend missed most from his homeland and it would be nice to surprise him next time we all met. The concertina never materialised, but the thought was there.

While Peter was at sixth form, he would occasionally take his pushbike on the train and travel to a library in Birmingham to study. On his return, he would tell us that he'd sat on the steps just listening to people who were down on their luck.

He was always gathering information and, for several years before he left for university, every day he used to read almost every newspaper – albeit they were usually a day old. The previous day's papers would be left in the officers' mess on the army base and Peter would pick them up after school each night.

This habit of reading all the newspapers was passed on to him, many years ago, by a man who said that he gained insight about a person by knowing what paper they read; and also that, by reading all the papers, he was able to talk to all people on all levels, quite apart from gaining a wide view of current affairs.

Recently Peter reminded me of the conversation he'd had with that man eighteen or so years ago. He said he hoped I never believed all the anthropological malarkey that I'd been told back then because, in fact, that man had only wanted to read page three of the *Sun*.

When he was about sixteen, the Bramcote Wives' Club (a club on the army base we were living on) were having a Military Skills Event and the ladies were given various tasks to do throughout the evening. As part of the event, there was a mock road-traffic accident designed to help assess first-aid skills. Volunteers were needed to play at being casualties and Peter volunteered to help out for the night. He was 'dressed' by the experts accordingly, mock injuries and lots of fake blood. He was such a realistic victim that some ladies treating him thought his wounds were real.

Happy, happy days — how can I select snapshots when there are just so many memories to recall? During his sixth-form years, Peter didn't have a Saturday job because he was always too busy, but he did have a Thursday job — which he detested. It involved delivering a free newspaper to each military home on the camp. I would prepare them for him, which meant stuffing any loose leaflets into the papers and folding them before placing them in his brightly coloured delivery bag. Each Thursday, he'd face a nagging session from me because he didn't want to do it — there were about 150 to 200 papers in all. Reluctantly, he would then set off and return at regular intervals to restock his bag. One day, I noticed that my stock of lollipops had suspiciously diminished and it wasn't long before I realised this was happening every Thursday. When I looked out across the road, there was a collection of children, each one with a lollipop in their mouth and papers under their arms. Peter would be entertaining them as they happily delivered the papers for him. The children loved Thursdays. The children loved Peter.

In June 1997, it came time for him to leave home following his A-levels. The family had a posting that would take us back to Germany in the August, so his plan was to work in London and to earn some money before going to university in September. He went to stay with his nanny and got a job digging graves. He said it would all be 'research' for later on. He couldn't wait to get to London and seemed – even before he went – to have a real feel for the city. But the same could also be said of Paris – George Orwell's thirties' novel, *Down and Out in Paris and London*, was one of his favourite books.

He stayed at his nan's flat for about six weeks before finding lodgings in a house not far away from her on the edge of Kilburn. He was under the watchful eye of his landlord, who, as luck would have it, was a social worker by profession. But we knew Peter was ready to spread his wings; we were too stifling for him at this point and he needed to get away from the boundaries we had set. It made his dad particularly sad, but both Peter senior and I understood. His sister was also in London at the time, and Peter became friendly with one of her pals from Brunel University – future fellow-Libertine Carl Barât.

Peter's love for London had developed from pouring over books, watching old black-and-white films such as *The Lavender Hill Mob* and *Passport to Pimlico*, listening to Chas & Dave songs and following his adored football club, QPR. He loved the many theatres and galleries, the vibrancy and the whole history of the place. I don't think though, he enjoyed those days of digging – it was hard work. He showed me his muscles!

Then, when September came, his dad's brother, John, moved Peter and all his belongings to his university digs and is still haunted by the lost look on Peter's face as he left him in the East End of London. John recalls how sad Peter had looked that day, and he hadn't wanted to leave him. When I phoned Peter to tell him his exam results before we left for Germany, he told me that he didn't want to go to university; that really he would like to earn some money and *find* himself. I asked him to reconsider this decision; that he had a wonderful life stretching out ahead of him, and that he might regret, in later life, not following up on the chance to go to college.

While at University, he would get involved in poetry events in and around London and once went to Russia on a visit arranged by the Arts Council. He told me he'd been asked to make a donation towards the cost but had no money and contributed a poem instead. Upon his return, he'd taken to wearing his most ridiculous headgear to date – an enormous Russian hat – and I remember being embarrassed when he wore it home.

On another occasion, he was invited to join a group of poets for a private party at London's Groucho Club. Peter, as the youngest poet there, felt both proud and privileged to have been asked. Nanny London has always said that Peter should give up his music and concentrate on his poetry. He has always written. When he was just ten years old I was called into school by his headmaster, told not to worry – that he wasn't in trouble – and asked for my permission to send Peter's work off to the education board. The head said it was an exceptional piece of writing for a child of his age.

Only the week before I had reprimanded Peter for writing lies – something I still do! He once told an NME reporter that he was one of fifteen children; another time he told them that he moved around a lot as a child – that he lived with his dad, his mum and the social workers. I was horrified.

For the piece he'd written at school, the class had been told to write about themselves and Peter had started with a line about his dad kicking a ball around in London and then taken the reader on a journey to Liverpool where I lived as a child, before bringing the story round to himself. For a child of his age it was very clever, but, as always, it was the truth mingled with his imagination.

However, although he was spreading his wings, Peter was still very involved with his family. As we moved about so much when the children were young, I was always concerned about them having to move schools often. I spoke about this to a head teacher who confided that he himself had been to thirteen schools – and he hadn't been part of the military. The key is to know your child, and our third child – Emily – clearly didn't like to change schools often. After considerable thought and soul searching, she went to boarding school as a rising twelve year old. Ironically, it was Peter junior who took this news badly. He phoned from university to ask me to reconsider. I assured him that Emily *wanted* to go (in as much as a child of that age can truly understand the consequences), but not until he'd been to look at the school did he let the subject lie. Peter was comforted by the fact that Emily wouldn't be starting alone but that her best friend at the time would also be going there.

It was whilst visiting that school that Peter sang me a song he was writing called 'Music When the Lights Go Out' – about a person trying to end a relationship. It made me cry. It is my favourite song of his today – that and 'Breck Road Lover' (Breck Road is a thoroughfare in Liverpool). He asked me if I liked 'Music When the Lights Go Out' and I said that I'd have been very happy if anyone had sung that when they were finishing with me because the lyrics would have softened the blow. It's a beautiful song and the words are pure poetry.

*

You may not have heard any of Peter's music at all. As his mother, I am obviously of a different generation, but I do actually like it and play his albums often – all of them. One song, 'For Lovers', which he made in collaboration with a local poet called Wolfman, is outstanding and haunting. As he's been in two bands – The Libertines and Babyshambles – there's a lot of music to listen to! When he used to come home, he would always have a guitar in his hand and I would say, 'Put that away.'

'Mum,' he'd say, 'people pay good money to hear me play.'

'Mmm, I'll pay you to stop.'

I can't believe I actually said that – it's a mother thing.

Even today, I'll ring when he's playing and he'll say, 'Oh, mum, please listen to this.' And I have to stop myself from saying, 'Don't bother.'

Peter's early music – some demos of which I have on CD from when he was in The Libertines – is wonderful and raw. They had a lot of talent and Peter, particularly, had a wonderful way with words. His dad thought that they had something special, too, and was very proud. But the next time I saw an album, it was full of songs about drugs. And when I saw the cover of The Libertines' second album (called *The Libertines*), which showed Peter and Carl looking at their tattoos, it looked as if Peter was showing his veins. I was mortified. I remember the first time I saw it was when

I was taking Lisa, Astile and his half-sister Molly home and we were driving into London. It was a summer's day and I had the roof down on my car as I drove over the Chiswick Flyover. Suddenly, there it was up on the billboards: what a sight for all the world to see!

Peter senior always liked the song, 'The Ha Ha Wall'. He thought that this number had great potential. I like almost everything that has been recorded. Once you can hear the words, the songs take on a new meaning.

Having been with Peter for nearly nine days in rehab number three – in May and June 2004 – and seeing him so ill, it was amazing to find that throughout all that time he was continually and copiously writing and composing. He would sing to me late into the night. I was shattered, truly. Eventually, one night, the nurse intimated that he would sleep. 'Oh, great!' I thought, but no such luck. Not only did I not get any sleep but also I had to dance and sing along until the early hours of the morning until, finally, Peter fell asleep exhausted. It was a long time coming!

On another night in the same rehab, Peter was sat up cross-legged in bed, writing his journals and gluing items of interest – photographs, letters from fans, drawings – into his books.

I said, 'Well this is a great Saturday night, son.'

Peter turned to me and said, 'This is rock 'n' roll.'

I looked at him, sat there in a Marks & Sparks dressing

gown with a hat on his head, a stick of glue in his hand and not a shoe to his name and just said, 'Yes, son, you look very rock 'n' roll.'

*

It's amazing to recall that he actually left home in June 1997. That's nine years ago. He was eighteen and on his way to university. He's now twenty-seven and on his way to who knows where.

I pray he makes it. For Pete's sake, I hope he makes it.

Chapter 8

Rumours Fly

Rumores volant

IF I AM honest with myself – and I do try really hard not to be – I have in many ways become an emotional cripple as I struggle to maintain my dignity, my sense of humour, and my sense of worth – although I try to give the illusion that everything is okay and that I can cope with whatever happens next.

Looking back on 2004, I'm left with a sense of wonder. I just don't know how I coped. Although I'm always one for asking questions, 'Are you using hard drugs? . . . Are you injecting?' were questions to which I couldn't bear to hear Peter's answer. It was easier not to ask . . . for a while, at least.

It was awful to discover, at some point during that year, that Peter had progressed (if that is the word to use) from *smoking* heroin to *injecting* it. I simply don't have the words to articulate how learning that Peter was injecting heroin affected me; perhaps only another parent in the same circumstances could fully understand. The very thought of being dependent on a chemical makes me feel sick. It makes me very angry. It makes me very sad. Injections don't bother me, I am a nurse . . . but injecting heroin into a vein leaves me cold. The thought that a child of mine could do this to themselves causes me to shudder. Why? Why? WHY?

The honest truth is that I don't even know when I first heard that this was the case because again it had slowly come to my attention through innuendoes. I remember asking people over a period of time if Peter was injecting and not getting any real answers. There were continual attempts by Peter and others throughout the year to try and modify his use; often he had endured self-induced withdrawal, such as when he came home for Christmas 2004. He was so ill – shaking, trembling, sweating, awful cramps, flu-like symptoms, unable to stand yet needing to use the bathroom often. And all this without the aid of anything to ease the symptoms.

At one point, he asked if there was any cranberry juice. I tenderly reassured him: 'Yes, the supermarket had a special offer – three cartons for two pounds – and I bought nine cartons.' Peter opened his eye and said 'Oh no, I can't drink that stuff. It's full of toxins – I only like the pure type.'

I just looked at him, unable to comprehend what I had just heard. Full of toxins? After what he'd been taking? He must be joking.

But he wasn't.

Normally we would all go to church as a family at Christmas but, by Christmas 2004, Peter was very unwell and in the throes of withdrawal. In fact, he did make it to the dinner table, but not for long. It was an awfully sad time – and yet an awfully happy time because he was alive and he was at home with us.

Peter, out of all the children, always enjoyed Christmas Eve – the thought of going to church late at night. He joined me once, as a young boy, and fell asleep. But he liked the idea. That particular Christmas Eve, though, I felt unable to leave the house knowing that it would take just one phone call and he'd be back in London; his feelings to stay would fight his feelings to go. In fact, he remarked on the fact that I hadn't gone to the midnight service. 'I'm not going anywhere,' he'd said to me as though he had read my thoughts. On Christmas morning, when it also became obvious that I wasn't going to church, he mocked me saying that I'd 'missed' the service and intimating, cheekily, that I would be in trouble with the Big One. No, this was not a day to be going to church; this was a day for doing the Christian thing and being where I could do God's work and just sit awhile.

Peter was with us for five days before we drove him back to London. He was desperate to return. He had made prior plans and we couldn't keep him against his will. A few days later, he had no less than five planned gigs up and down the country on one night, New Year's Eve.

My husband had been wonderful throughout that whole Christmas episode and he and Peter talked long into the night, amid tears and well-intended promises on both parts to fight this destructive and overwhelming problem head on. Peter senior took some leave a few weeks later and headed for London to spend time with Peter. I was worried about the whole thing and joked that he wouldn't last twenty-four hours; one-to-one time with Peter is a great part of the Peter Problem because it is so rare and, indeed, this day was to be no different.

I was so proud of my two boys and after leaving them in London with food — odd delicacies that they both enjoy and a whole home-cooked ham — I felt so happy. I was looking forward to going to bed that night. Peter was with his dad, and I hoped that, finally, I would get a good night's sleep. I think I even switched off my mobile, such was the belief that all would be well.

But it wasn't to be. My husband hadn't managed to stay with Peter for the whole twenty-four hours after all. I awoke from a deep sleep at four o'clock in the morning to hear the downstairs phone ringing and leapt to pick up the receiver, knowing that this could only mean trouble. It was deeply disappointing to learn that Peter senior was at Victoria Coach Station, having dragged his small case from Islington across London in the cold, unrelenting January air to secure a seat on the first means of transport out of London. Replacing the receiver, I called Peter's number but there was no reply. I knew that if big Pete was feeling upset then little Peter would be also. Later that morning, I picked up my husband from Poole; but no sooner had he arrived home than he decided that he had reacted badly and that he would go back to London and try all over again.

He returned to London the following day and stayed at his mother's place in Cricklewood, before travelling across the city to find Peter and make a fresh start. This time it was easier said than done. Peter is not one for staying in one place for too long – an interview here, an afternoon gig there; it would take a Philadelphia lawyer to keep tabs on his activities. There were people in Peter's flat that my husband didn't know, so he eventually made his way back to his mother's house and, after a few more failed attempts at locating his son, he returned to Dorset devastated, defeated and overwhelmingly discouraged. My husband felt so bad. I can't explain his pain. He probably wouldn't be able to explain it himself – his is a father's pain.

It is irrelevant to me that other musicians have trodden this path before because everybody's story is different. This makes no difference to a mother's heart. It certainly doesn't ease the pain.

Over the years there have always been attempts by Peter to address his problems and many other people have tried to help. To mention some would be unfair because there have been so many and I'd end up leaving out some who have truly tried hard to make a difference. But I heartily thank each of them; they know who they are.

*

Peter began 2005 with a chest infection that laid him low for a few days. He moved in to a newly built apartment and my husband and I drove up to London on a Saturday in mid-January to spend some time with him. We found him well and in good spirits. The flat was nice and clean – if a little sparse due to the fact that he had just moved in and not yet made an impression upon the place – and he was positive and felt that things were going well. Peter looked fine. We didn't stay very long as he was dashing around, about to travel up to Oxford to sing, that same evening, at the birthday party of the model Kate Moss. Peter mixed in different circles from us and knew lots of celebrities. We promised to return the following week with tea towels, bookshelves and kitchen utensils. It was a positive visit. We headed off to visit relatives and he headed off to Oxford.

If the press had hounded us before this day then nothing could have prepared us for the onslaught afterwards. Purely because of Peter and Kate's association, suddenly the phone was ringing non-stop, letters were arriving, extended family members were door-stepped and my mother-in-law was being harassed daily.

There were so many things happening in early 2005 – court case after court case, arrest after arrest, utter mayhem. Peter was stalked by fans, followed by film crews recording his every move, 'papped' by opportunists. It was all getting out of hand. So much was going on in our lives, and in Peter's life, that every day was a huge challenge.

However, there are some incidents that stick in my mind.

In February 2005, there was the moment when one of Peter's security men told me that a photographer had offered him £60,000 for a photo of Peter and Kate together. He said that, as the person walked away, another opportunist had approached him upping the previous offer to £100,000. It's unbelievable – and *very* sick.

At this point, Peter had security guards to protect him from people who were trying to get drugs to him, to protect him from himself. They were very kind to me. As his troubles were spiralling out of control again – this time involving someone who had made a documentary about him and who had allegedly sold a newspaper photographs of Peter smoking heroin – there was a window of opportunity to get him into a rehab again. I don't know how this came about, but once again I travelled up from Dorset to be with him and, whilst I was with him, he made the decision to have an implant.

An implant is usually surgically placed in the stomach or leg just beneath the skin. It releases Naltrexalone which blocks nerve transmitters in the brain and spine and prevents heroin, if then taken, having any effect. There are dangers: should an addict then take a further dose of heroin in the hope of its having an effect, they run a high risk of death. There are also other problems. On its own, an implant has limited benefits; further problems can arise if the addict's patterned behaviour, triggers, thought processes, habits, change of lifestyle and other obvious issues –

such as an increasing use of other substances — are not addressed at the same time. Furthermore, it can only be expected to work for six months.

A moving incident that I will never forget, and which also involves money, occurred late one night, in the small hours. The phone rang. It was a voice I didn't recognise; a troubled voice. 'Here we go,' I remember thinking. 'Hello, who's there?'

The voice was tentative, asking whether I was Peter's mother. She told me how she had obtained my number and apologised for calling me so late but said that it was a call that she had to make. I have an over-active imagination and dreaded what was coming next. She told me she was an addict and had little money and that she really wanted me to know that the press had approached her and offered her money (not very much either) to tell a 'story' about Peter. She said that she had never met Peter, but that he was a friend of a friend of a friend. She said that she needed the money badly but had done the right thing and had declined the offer of telling a 'story' that wouldn't have been true. Before I could say another thing she had put the receiver down. She, too, was some mother's prodigal child.

February 2005 saw rehab number five and brought with it the first implant, performed in London, and instigated by Peter himself — with the thought, the belief, the hope that this would really help. In many ways, I suppose it did. There was indeed a difference in his behaviour, he was glad to be free of his dependency on heroin, he was in love and Babyshambles were doing well.

Babyshambles. It has been a concern of mine that the mothers of the other young men in the band may worry about their own sons being associated with Peter; perhaps they are petrified at what they read or hear. But these are lovely young men, as were the rest of The Libertines.

The Babyshambles drummer, Adam Ficek, was a teacher in a former life. Sadly, his mother died and I have never had the opportunity to speak with her. I have spoken to the mother of bass player Drew McConnel, and look forward to meeting her one day soon.

Whenever I travelled to visit Peter, I usually took the train from Dorset to London. My beautiful grandson Astile had been photographed for a poster advertisement when he was only a few months old and, at one time, his face had been in almost every London street, on London buses and in stations. Even now, his picture is still up in Woking station wearing a red and white striped top. He's bald and toothless.

Normally, when leaving Waterloo to return home, I would be tearful over having to leave Peter in London – the usual battle of head versus heart – not having stayed longer and feeling that I'd failed to make any difference. But always, as the train pulls into Woking and I see Astile's picture, I stop crying momentarily. Often I'd text his mother: 'Peter may be *down* in *Albion* but Astile is Up in Woking' – a reference to a song Peter had written entitled 'Albion' and the first Babyshambles album which was called *Down in Albion*. I usually want to shout to the whole carriage: 'That is *my* grandson,' but I usually just shed a few silent saline drops and remain silent.

A funny thing happened to me on the way to Peter's on his twenty-sixth birthday. It was a Saturday and he was on curfew – a court ruling relating to his ongoing court case – so I knew if I got there early enough, he would be in. I had warned him that I'd be up to have a jig with him and to sing 'Happy Birthday'. All had been planned and I reminded and reminded Peter, even up to the night before, that I was coming, but I knew that this would make no difference as to whether or not he would actually be there. Plans can change on a sixpence where Peter is concerned. Make plans, but be flexible, have a good knowledge of the underground and, most important, wear a comfortable pair of shoes.

I rose at 3 a.m., drove to Salisbury, then took the first train to London at 5.15 a.m., meandered my way across London by tube to as near to Peter's house as it could deliver me, then began collecting daffodils – several bunches, not yet opened to face the world. Here was I, a mother who'd risen in the middle of the night to spend some time with an evasive son, muttering a few long-forgotten lines of William Wordsworth's poem: 'I Wandered Lonely As a Cloud . . .'

Walking on through London as the smaller shops were just opening, nipping into a well-placed supermarket, picking up some favourite food for the birthday boy – a chocolate gateau – and then on to his apartment, thinking perhaps I should ring to say that I was ten minutes away.

'Hi, it's mum. I'm passing a bakery, a wonderful-smelling shop. How many people are with you in the flat?'

'Oh, I'm just on my way to the studio, there's a car waiting outside,' said a surprised Peter.

'Don't move . . . I'll jump in a taxi and be there in three minutes,' I said, the shocked mother, having come thus far and knowing that if he left the apartment I'd be tracking him down all day.

I bought loads of sausage rolls, bacon rolls, sausage and bacon rolls combined, and still had just under half a cup of black coffee left, so sipping it I hailed a taxi. I gave the street name but, as I was clambering into the back of a black cab armed with rolls, cakes, cards, presents, daffodils and my coffee, the cabbie told me that I was under no circum-stances getting into his cab with an alcoholic drink. I tried hard to explain that it was coffee but he sped off. I gulped the last of the drink down, hailed another cab and cried all the way to Peter's flat.

The once-clean apartment was in utter disarray, transformed into a type of chaos, although not without its obvious charm and creativity – and of course the ubiquitous 'reading couch'. We jigged as I gave my rendition of 'Happy Birthday'. The daffs were banished to empty champagne bottles, I shared out the rolls as several people moved stealthily about the room, leaving Peter and I alone for less than a few minutes during which time I tried to offer deep, meaningful words of advice, realising they were all ready to leave for rehearsal. Peter asked if I wanted to come, he offered me a lift, invited me to the studio, tempting me with an offer of lunch. But, thirty minutes after I'd arrived at the flat, I was 'discharged', albeit gently, onto the street from whence I had arrived – not, however, before I'd surreptitiously placed on his table a copy of 'Our Daily Bread' a booklet of daily devotionals which I always leave dotted around the place in the hope he may pick it up.

It wasn't even ten o'clock and I was on my way back to deepest, darkest Dorset. I had planned for a few hours alone with Peter, at the very least. With no heart to hail another taxi, I walked uncomfortably to Angel station to catch the tube. I would gaze upon the innocent countenance of my grandson at Woking, instead.

My hope at this time was that the implant he'd had would work. And he'd done it voluntarily, which I felt was a positive step. Still, I thought, how on earth did it get to this? An implant to stop him taking heroin. I still find it unbelievable. It happens all the time that, when I'm faced with the reality of the problems Peter has today, some memory of the past will pop up in such a way that leaves me looking for an answer as to how it all began. What had gone wrong? Was there anything we could possibly have changed?

Other parents with addictive children tell me the same thing. They are always going over the child's life, and looking for pointers to indicate that there could be a problem, and wondering how they missed them.

*

I had never been to the Glastonbury Music Festival, nor had I ever had the remotest desire to go. But once I heard that Peter would be playing there in June 2005, I thought I would pop over to see him – it wasn't far from home – never wanting to miss a chance to see his band if they were remotely near. I wasn't on duty at work so I had no excuse not to go.

According to everyone around me, this was an opportunity I shouldn't miss – quite apart from the fact my son was performing. My husband's cousin Carol would escort me and we were both very excited. Carol couldn't sleep beforehand. She and her hubby, Barry, are big fans of Babyshambles and follow their every move. My boss, who has been a wonderful support to me, had checked the weather at Glastonbury over that period and assured me that it wasn't going to rain.

The previous week I had been rummaging through clothes in an attempt to find suitable attire. I needed something with plenty of pockets – the more the better. Carol and I were about to set off when I noticed she was wearing a smart pair of Hunter wellingtons and she then handed me a pair of Dunlops. I don't do wellies. I was never a Brownie or a Girl Guide because my mother made me go dancing instead; I grew up in the age of Shirley Temple when all mothers sent their daughters to tap and ballet. Both my girls were Brownies and Guides and Peter was a Beaver Cub and a Cub Scout. Nevertheless, my motto is always to 'Be prepared', so I took the wellies ungratefully, begrudgingly and horrified that they were green and I had nothing to match them. Just as well that I did – four minutes into our journey and the heavens opened. However, even as we arrived, early, sodden down one side because my car roof had a small leak, it became obvious that it would take more than a torrential downpour to dampen these revellers. I, however, found it very hard to exit my leaking car and sat there wearing a black bin liner.

I wanted to text my boss to tell her not to give up her day job for a future in weather forecasting. 'No rain over Glastonbury . . .' her words echoed in my ear. I would have texted her but a lightning strike meant that mobile phones wouldn't work.

We sat silently and I wanted to go home – to my nice dry home – but knew that I had to stop complaining, put the wellies on and enjoy myself. Nothing can prepare you for the experience. The queues to get in, the parking, the haemorrhaging of people from vehicles, the orderliness, the lack of expletives, the kindness of total strangers – and that was just the first few minutes, but it lasted throughout.

Peter wasn't arriving until much later and neither Carol nor I had a clue where to go or what to do. Glastonbury 2005 was like a city under the sea. We passed one submerged tent after another — even floating tents. We had tickets for the weekend but had no intention of staying overnight. Being the raver that I am, I thought it prudent to go home at night, get a good sleep, and return the next day.

We did see Babyshambles and they were great. Peter had arrived seconds before they were due on stage, adding to the tension. He and Kate had been caught up in heavy traffic all the way down. As their performance ended, Carol and I made our way to the backstage area to meet Peter. As he posed for the cameras, signed autographs and took a beer passed to him by a fan, he caught sight of me and called me to him.

Peter asked me whether I had any water and, as I didn't, led me over to the hospitality tent. There was a young lady on the 'door' who wouldn't let him in. 'This is for performers only,' she said. Peter could see that I was about to say something along the lines of, 'He has just come off stage,' but he stopped me. 'Leave it, mum,' he said. 'She's doing her job.' Instead, we went to his nearby tour bus for a drink. This is the very gentle, caring side of Peter that I witness often. After a short period of time I left him, not wanting to embarrass him and knowing, too, that we both had so much to explore at Glastonbury.

Before we parted company, Carol took a few photographs of Peter and I together. He seemed well but let me know that he was going to be frantically busy with gigs and commitments over the ensuing weeks. We left open any plans to meet up again. We'd make contact by phone. I was invited to join him and the band but I never really feel comfortable hanging around Peter, always thinking that he needs to get on with his life and not have his mother watching his every move.

Driving home late that night, I had a head full of memories, a heart full of a mother's love and there were very few parts of my apparel that didn't have mud ingrained. I was as muddy as one could possibly be with blisters too painful even to look at – but I was happy.

That didn't last long. Suddenly, my car didn't seem able to get up hills and had lost its oomph. I ended up being towed home by the Automobile Association because the clutch had gone. A memorable night indeed.

A frosty reception greeted me when I arrived home: my husband was not best pleased that I had gone to Glastonbury. I think he felt that my going gave a subliminal message that I condoned the 'rock 'n' roll lifestyle' and all that goes with that image. Nothing could be further from the truth. I'll repeat again, for the record, I abhor drugs of *any* class.

Despite how Peter senior felt, Carol and I returned to the festival the next day and, that night, we went backstage before the Babyshambles gig and chatted with some lovely people who seemed to go out of their way to make us feel comfortable. The minute Peter arrived he was mobbed. He asked if I wanted to watch from the side of the stage to get a good view but I wanted to see them from the audience and then just slip away home.

The whole Glastonbury experience was amazing and I know we didn't have nearly enough time to see everything. I had gone there kicking and screaming, not really wanting to go, but had left in much the same manner – not really wanting to leave. It was superb. Even for me, with the weight of an addicted son on my heart and the knowledge that his implant was in its penultimate month, these had been two memorable days. Two good days.

Chapter 9

What a Waste!

Vincit qui se vincit – He conquers
who conquers himself

TOWARDS THE END of 2005, Peter was talking more and
more about going to a rehabilitation clinic in Arizona –
this would be rehab number six. I recalled that erudite man
at a previous clinic suggesting this may just be the very place
where Peter should go. Peter had failed in previous attempts
to travel to rehab in the States – sometimes he simply hadn't
made the flight – but I eventually received the wonderful
news that he had actually left England and was on his way to
Arizona.

I cried. I prayed. I danced. I thanked God. I rang and
thanked a lot of people. I half packed a suitcase, awaiting
word for when I would be able to visit him. I had never
been across the Atlantic. The family were unbelievably
thrilled. This would be the one, we all thought. This would

be the catalyst that would turn his life around.

The following Monday, 28 November, was Emily's birthday and Peter called me from Arizona to ask for her number so he could call to wish her a happy birthday. How sweet, I thought. I was ecstatic.

'How are you?' I asked him. 'When am I allowed to visit?'

'I will call you again to discuss that, have to go now,' he said. Was that an alarm bell beginning to ring in my head?

I called and spoke to Jeanette Lee at Rough Trade, having already agreed that whoever heard from him first would call the other. We were both so happy. But as the day wore on, and the excitement diminished, I could hear those alarm bells ringing louder and louder. Why did he have a mobile phone with him? The clinic always takes mobile phones away as routine practice.

I rang Jeanette with panic in my voice and told her something wasn't right. She said she'd try to find out what was going on, and call back if she had any news. Meanwhile, I went about my normal routine and berated myself for being so suspicious.

In the past, Peter has told me that I have a suspicious mind. I can't argue with that but I prefer to think of it as a sensitivity, a second sense. Admittedly, it's sometimes a case of me adding two and two and getting five. Oh, God knows how I wished I was wrong in this instance.

For any parent or, in fact, anyone with a loved one suffering from an addiction of any description, there comes a numbing of the pain when they go into rehab. Hope swells up and a feeling of relief washes over you. Will this be the rehab in which it all clicks into place? Over and above the different emotions that you experience, you feel that tonight, at least, they are safe. You can sleep easily, knowing, believing and hoping that no harm can come to them – at least for one night.

On the Wednesday, I was at work when a colleague told me she had read in the paper that Peter had left Arizona. She must be wrong, I thought. I would have heard. I tried to call the rehab centre but they wouldn't release any information: the nurse on duty kept saying that she was not at liberty to confirm or deny that Peter had even been there, never mind whether he'd discharged himself. My boss was by my side as I made my final appeal:

'Please, I am his mother and the papers are saying that he's been sighted in London. I just need to know the truth.'

'Bless your heart,' she said, sympathetically, but repeated the set answer.

I was none the wiser.

Shortly afterwards, Geoff Travis from Rough Trade called me. He had it on good authority that Peter had been in London the previous night. He then told me to brace myself for even worse news. What could be worse than this, I thought? Peter had been arrested again.

This recurring bad news was having an effect on me. I could hardly lift up my head, I felt so low. The nightmare was on replay. It was like *Groundhog Day*, the film in which

Bill Murray keeps waking to the same day, over and over and over . . .

To say that I can fully understand why and how Marvin Gaye's father had killed his son seems rather dramatic, but the fact is that I do understand. When you have brought your child up to know the difference between right and wrong, and then you have to stand by and see that child suffer and stumble brings trouble to a parent's heart. It doesn't matter that he's a grown man; a parent feels the terrible burden of blame and guilt upon them. That is the bottom line. I have even told Peter that was how I felt. I have said to him, and to my colleagues, how a dose of insulin would be just the ticket to stop the madness. It would put the Peter Problem to sleep for ever. It would kill him. What an awful thing to think and I'm not proud for thinking it, I'm ashamed. I say it out loud to act as a safety device – to express how low I'm feeling. To voice that sentiment is, I think, very low indeed, but that's how I feel at times. And I think all mothers feel like this when they have addictive children.

This latest episode of Peter running from rehab knocked me for six. The tears flowed as I unpacked my suitcase. Hope ebbed away.

This was an all-time low for me. It was just before Christmas and there were difficulties at home. Peter's dad had said that he was no longer allowed to come home. But if I felt low, then it was doubly hard for my poor husband.

He was no longer 'living', he was just getting through the day – and not getting through it very well, either. Sheer professionalism alone kept him going, and still does. He is a soldier and he has to go to work. It wouldn't occur to him to take time off for stress. I have the same work ethic. I actually believe that going to work helps; it's a reason to get out of bed in the morning, when all you want to do is go to sleep and not wake up. It wasn't a case of suicidal thoughts but just a desire to have some peace and not have to live in the way we were doing now.

When I was a young student nurse, it was part of our teaching that our personal life didn't interfere with our work: once your uniform was on, you concentrated on the job in hand. This ethic has been beneficial to me these past three years.

There is every facility in the army available twenty-four-seven to help any soldier that needs it, but who could help Peter's father with this? Who does a once-proud man ask for help? I know of so many families who are ripped apart by lesser problems. My husband was a broken man. He still is. We are a broken family.

How were we going to get through Christmas? I took great comfort from the fact that Peter would be seeing Astile on this special day – I felt better that he should see his son than I see mine.

One day – it was a Friday – shortly before Christmas 2005 when things were very bad at home and the Peter Problem was raging, my husband very quietly but very pointedly asked me to do him a favour. He wanted to be alone. He asked me to leave the family home for a week, to book into a hotel – anything – but to leave him alone. He asked if I could leave before he returned from work.

He asked so quietly, yet so precisely, that it made me very frightened. Not frightened for me but afraid for my husband. I felt that he had reached his nadir and so I didn't argue. He felt that I understood. Once he had left for work, I cried and prayed. My husband has no faith; nothing to support him or to bring him hope or comfort.

I made two phone calls – one to the padre on camp because I was scared that my husband would commit suicide, and one to a friend called Liz to ask whether she had a spare bed for a few nights. After packing my bag, I left a note for Peter senior saying where I would be and to call me anytime. I am a crier, but this time I cried a river.

I was only out of the house for two days. I returned home on the Sunday. Peter senior had called me and said that I'd better come home. Here was a man unable to sleep, severely distressed and at a loss as to what to do. It doesn't get much worse than this. When I write the Peter Problem it now takes on another meaning, the Peter (plural) Problem.

If you have ever seen the film *The Jazz Singer* then you will understand. It was easier for the father in the film to say his son was dead than to have to bear the pain of accepting the way his son was living. It isn't quite that bad in our situation, but the pain is as great.

In 1993, aged 14, Peter made his first public appearance singing karaoke at a wedding. It was a Beatles song and he was out of tune the whole way through. No crowd surfing, then, but plenty of crowd squirming.

Peter on holiday in the Med.

The camera *does* lie. Peter taking part in a road traffic accident training session, part of a Wives' Club military skills event.

'So tell me, Grandad, what do you really think about this prawn cocktail?' Aged 16, enjoying Christmas with the family.

Peter chills out in his own world.

Peter and Emily welcome AmyJo back from university in their own inimitable way.

Peter, aged 17, taken by his dad near our house in Bramcote.

Peter the minstrel, home for the 1998 Christmas holidays…

…and dressed for dinner.

Having a jig with me, Christmas 1999.

A twenty-year-old Peter,
taken at the flat he shared
with Carl in Camden.

Posing for the camera.
Peter with his dad,
enjoying Christmas 2000.

Oh no! Not another Libertine! Astile, Peter's son, aged two-and-a-half, at Nanny and Grandad's house.

Peter with his beloved Nanny London.

A very different
Christmas scene
in 2002.

Peter and AmyJo.
Christmas 2002. Wildenrath
Germany

In fact, this pain is off the scale and there is no analgesia that can lessen it because it pervades the whole of your being. It's there when you try to get to sleep and is still there when you wake. Pain for me is a signal that something is not right; the dictionary describes it as being an unpleasant sensation, occurring in varying degrees of severity, as a result of injury, disease or emotional disorder. However you describe it, it hurts.

Although I had returned home, nothing had changed. Peter senior had moved himself into the spare room and, as much as this was very upsetting for me, it actually gave me the space and ability to keep my phone switched on during the night. I hardly slept and my husband barely slept; I could hear him walking around at night. There was dialogue between us but things were strained. There were only four or five weeks to go until Christmas and I continued preparing for the 'festivities' as always.

I am notorious among my friends for sending early Christmas cards, largely because we move house so regularly and it ensures that people have a correct address for me. I enjoy keeping in touch with the many friends that I have made over the years, even if it is only once a year.

Eventually Peter senior and I were able to thrash out some issues. He found the whole Peter Problem so very hard to tolerate but understood on a deep level that for my part, as a mother, I had to continue along the lines of keeping in touch with Peter, had to continue to hope, continue to have faith. The only thing left to do, it seemed at the time, was to consider ending our marriage as we knew it because, as far as Peter senior was concerned my involvement with my son made it intolerable. You may think the obvious – that this was a choice for me: either my husband or my son. But that wasn't the case. I don't have a choice. One is my son and I am unable to turn my back on him even though I have wanted to at times; the other is my husband to whom I made a solemn vow – for better or for worse, until death us do part. He can leave me, but I can't leave him.

When the going has been tough, how I have wished that I didn't feel the solemnity of those vows; vows that were thrust upon me when I didn't even ask to make them. I was perfectly happy having had a civil ceremony in a registry office. However, when the garrison's padre learned that I hadn't made my marital vows in front of the altar, he arranged – with the matron of my nursing unit – that Peter senior and I should be married in church forthwith. Why had the padre and the matron gone to such lengths to ensure that my marriage was blessed? I now believe that it was for times such as these.

It would have been too easy not to give a second thought to breaking my vows. I am an independent person and my inner happiness has never depended upon someone else or my set of circumstances. My inner happiness has largely been contentment in all things; in the good and the bad, knowing who I am, knowing what I can change and what I can't and accepting all situations.

Remember, however, that this was also the time that Peter junior had made his latest escape from rehab in Arizona. His leaving this rehab caused me to move to a new place. I was angry. No other word for it. And if I could have tracked him down I would really have given him a piece of my mind. I'm not one given to losing my temper, but this latest bolt from what seemed like the ideal situation had hit me hard. So much so that we had no contact for almost a week, normally I would have been ringing around, chasing him up but I just felt overwhelmed and needed some time and space to gather some strength again, the Peter (x2) Problems were raging and seemed insurmountable.

It was clear that there would be no Christmas celebrations in our home and I was told not to bother even cooking a Christmas dinner. Nor to expect a Christmas present, these things weren't spoken in anger or with malice. They didn't even particularly upset me, I was already too upset to be upset. It was pointless arguing – but I do remember standing my ground and quietly saying that Christmas was the one time of the year that was special to me, evoking memories of years gone by and giving me hope for the years to come. As a woman of faith in these modern days, in truth every day is 'Christmas' for me. I don't need an over-commercialised period to focus my mind on the true Christmas message, but I do actually enjoy the whole Christmas thing.

My daughters were due home and arrived the day before Christmas Eve, so how on earth could I get around this –

cancelling Christmas would break their hearts. It was bad enough that their brother wouldn't be home. The answer was quite simple: I would book them a holiday in the sun, Emily had been two when we left Cyprus and had no memory of it and I was able to secure, for the festive period, a week in a four-star Hotel.

In truth, I'd have liked to go with them and it did cross my mind to do just that, but I wasn't really in holiday mode and felt I might well have just ruined things for them. The other reason that I felt I should stay home was for big Pete, I couldn't bear the thought of him being alone, even though that was what he had wanted.

It wasn't all doom and gloom, though. I remained as cheerful as I could and put up a tree, wrapped gifts, made six dozen mince pies, sang around the house and played happy music. Big Pete even helped with the lights and, because our grandson was coming to stay for a few days, he also decorated the outside of our home. Everything looked normal to the outsider and, in some strange way, we were coping. There was no animosity. There was no rush to end the marriage.

Before leaving the house on Christmas morning, to take the girls to the airport, my husband gave me the most beautiful present — it was an antique silver bracelet that he had especially sourced for me. It made me cry inside as he had told me previously not to expect any present that year, and here I had been given a most poignant reminder of his love for me. This was no ordinary bracelet. For me it was a true love token. By most people's standards, it may not have cost a great deal, but this exquisite piece of jewellery had antique silver Christian symbols, antique Austrian crystals and he had spent a lot of time looking for it. He could never know how precious it was for me to be given this gift at this time.

At 8 a. m. on Christmas morning I was driving AmyJo and Emily to Bristol airport for their holiday flight when Peter Junior called to wish them Merry Christmas. We all exchanged pleasantries; we all cried. We like to be together at Christmas. The family tradition is that we go to church as a family on Christmas morning – even my husband! – and that we wait until after church to open our presents.

I had made a large Christmas meal the night before and there were plenty of leftovers. By choice, my husband spent the day alone. He wanted it that way. For most of our married life, we have always had a busy Christmas day. Although my parents are now dead, they regularly came to us for the holiday period and my husband would always invite people who were alone – through work commitments or otherwise – to join us for dinner. In thirty years of marriage, we have only had two Christmases alone – the first was in the first year of our marriage and I was on duty in casualty, and the second was the year after when, again, I was on duty and my husband was on fire-fighting duty in South Wales during the firemen's strike of 1977. Ever since then, we have always squashed in as many people as possible around our table.

As I drove home late that Christmas afternoon, happy that, at the very least, my husband had his long-awaited peace, that my daughters were on their way to an adventure and that Peter was with his son Astile, I myself was feeling very worn, tired and quite unwell. It was okay though – I could be ill now. As I arrived home I had every intention of just going to bed but as I entered the house was warmly greeted by big Pete and discovered that he had prepared dinner for the two of us and I was beginning to think that we would come through this after all. The Christmas Miracle.

I have no doubt of the love my husband has for me. I also have no doubt that he would like to distance himself from the problems that we now find ourselves in. This is a time in our lives when we should be able to sit back a bit after a lifetime of service and enjoy ourselves a little. Nowadays, I have no idea what the future is bringing for us. I take each day as it comes.

A couple of years ago Emily and I met Peter for breakfast. It was actually meant to be a solemn affair as he was in the grip of his addiction and the press was full of awful stories. I was trying to prepare myself for what we might have to face; I had papers with me for him to sign so that his affairs would be in order should the worst occur. Emily was eighteen and now fully aware of what was happening – what we hadn't told her she had read in the press. We couldn't possibly protect her anymore; it was something that we all had to deal with as a family.

It was a beautiful morning and we breakfasted outside in a lovely place opposite where Peter was living in a part of London that he adores. He showed me old bookshops and blue plaques on houses in which famous people had once lived. It was very difficult to believe he was an addict; he was so gentle. All the time we sat and ate, Peter was asked for autographs and photos. Eventually I braced myself to show him the documents he knew I was bringing.

He looked them over.

'You think I'm going to die don't you?' he asked.

'Yes, son, I do,' I admitted.

After breakfast he whisked us off to a shop in Covent Garden that specialises in vintage clothing because he was on tour that night and needed a suit. As we entered the shop, I saw the shop assistants nudge each other and one of them (a charming man) seemed to know exactly what Peter was looking for. Whilst he was trying on a suit, I saw one I really liked: I often picked up interesting items for him as I share his passion for second-hand clothes. 'I like this one,' I said, but the man walked over and told me rather disparagingly: 'Peter won't like that – it has three buttons and he only likes two buttons.'

What did I know?

'It's a fab suit though – what's the difference?' I asked.

'A button,' Peter quipped from behind the tastefully draped curtain.

He left the shop with two suits, shirts, ties, hats and had hardly spent what most people would spend on a single cheap suit. Sadly though, he had no shoes as they didn't have his size. Peter is a size twelve and he'd thrown his shoes into the crowd the night before. He only had baseball boots with him, so we spent the rest of the day walking up and down the streets of Covent Garden, in and out of shops, looking for a large pair of shoes but to no avail. I still have his very first pair of shoes ever. A brown pair.

It was prophetic, perhaps, that Peter once sang a song called 'What a Waster . . .'

My version would be 'What a waste'.

Chapter 10

Everyone Wants a Story

**Quis, Quid, Ubi, Quomondo, Quando? –
Who, What, Where, How, When?**

'Everyone wants a story'

Everyone wants to know
But for me there is no glory
In his own words, a 'horror show'

People praise the talent
And want to play their part
But I've always known his promise
It's been there from the start

It's always been within him
So big – it couldn't hide
But since his so-called 'success'
Something else has died

At first a REAL libertine
So free and then so true
But then he found a different scene
And I lost that boy I knew

He never heeded warnings
He was plucked so fresh and ripe
As the devil took his liberty
And swapped it for a pipe

He thought he was above it
That he could never lose
And at first of course, did enjoy it
Until he could no longer choose

The arrogance of youth then
the price some pay for fame
It's such a common thing in the industry
but even there I can't lay blame

Of course I'm proud and I love him
But now the whole world wants a piece
admirers, reporters, celebrity whores
so called 'friends', drug dealers, the police

The achievement loses all glory
Our family ruined by crack and by smack
I'd sell them a million stories
If they could give my brother back
AmyJo Doherty, 2005

My son has a fantastic sense of humour – a real gift for a quip; a quick wit indeed. As a child he would play tricks on his grandad who would fall for them every time.

My father, Percy Michels, the youngest of seven children, was a Liverpool cab driver. Percy's father, Maurice, was a French Jew, and his mother, Chana, whom I never met, was originally from Russia. She and her sister had escaped the troubles in her own country before the turn of the twentieth century and had fled to France. She married Maurice and they had a good life there before going to England where he was commissioned to oversee the building of a bridge in his professional capacity as an engineer, I think. Their new home was in Bedford Street, Liverpool, where they moved into a large, thirteen-room house (which no longer exists today).

Chana and Maurice had one daughter, Dinah, and six sons: Oscar, Bartholomew, Charles, Michael, Antoine, and Paris – my dad – who would later change his name to Percy. However, by the time Chana had given birth to my father, Maurice had left her – running off to France with their maid. Chana spoke no English and the money she had didn't last long. She took to renting out some of the rooms in the house in order to survive. All the children were bi-lingual. All, except my father, were well educated. And all the children embraced the Jewish faith – except for young Paris.

One of his brothers, Tony – so the family story goes – spoke eleven languages fluently, and my dad used to tell me that he had been an interpreter for General de Gaulle in Algiers. Whether it's true or not I have no idea but, when I was eight or nine years old, I went to meet him at Liverpool's Lime Street Station and all the press were there. He was wearing a very grand uniform and lived in Lyons until he died.

When war came, all the boys were enlisted in the French Army – except Paris. Peter's grandfather was called up to serve in the British Army and, at eighteen, he changed his name from Paris Michels to Percy Paris Michels. I once asked him why he'd pick a name like Percy and he told me that, at school – he'd attended King David's, a school in Liverpool – he never learned much because he never paid attention. However, during English history he'd heard of the House of Percy and thought it a fine English name.

During the war, my dad was stationed in Italy. He served in Monty's Eighth Army and had been part of the North Africa campaign (the Desert Rats) in the then Royal Service Corps, at some point working as the driver for the Commanding Officer. Shortly before returning to England, en route from Italy at the end of the war, he spent some time in Paris where he explained to his C.O. that he had never met his father and believed him to be in France. He was granted a twenty-four-hour pass and set off to track down Maurice. He later told me that, when he found him, he told him off in four languages for having left his mother. He had known his father was an educated man and wanted to show him that he, too, could speak in several tongues.

Peter loved his grandad; they used to have such a laugh, telling jokes and making them up. Peter used to hide his Dictaphone and then lure Percy into deep conversations. Often he would ask something like: 'You can tell me grandad, what do you *really* think of nanny's hair (or mum's cooking)?' Grandad's relayed answers would cause huge ructions. Peter would also phone his grandad on the mobile phone Percy used for long-distance taxi jobs and book him for long jobs, using a different accent each time. It was just the funniest thing. My dad fell for it every time.

My dad died in 1998. He would be heartbroken if he could see his grandson now. Ironically, it was to Peter that he left his prized possession when he died – his gold Jewish star. I flew over from Germany on the day he died and AmyJo and Peter travelled up to Liverpool from their digs in London. I had been left as executor of his estate and, in a written instruction, he had said that Peter was to have his gold Star of David. By the time Peter had arrived in Liverpool for the funeral, I had noticed another member of the family wearing the star and gently pointed out the instruction to both parties. It was a potentially tricky situation. I told Peter that it was his decision alone – his grandad had wanted him to have it, after all, therefore it was legally his. His uncle, all credit to him removed the star and handed it to Peter. Peter took it. Then, in a gentle and humble manner, Peter told everyone present that, yes, the star was his; then he turned to his uncle and, handing back the star, asked whether he could possibly look after it for him. I was so proud of the way he handled it.

That night Peter slept in his grandad's bed – in which Percy had died that very morning (the sheets, of course, had been changed). The next morning, he came downstairs in his grandad's dressing gown.

So much rubbish is written about Peter having had a strict army upbringing, but it is just that – utter rubbish. He was a happy child; he was a happy baby, and I can't honestly ever remember Peter being moody or sad.

He expressed his opinions: when, at a young age, he decided that he no longer wanted to go to church, I respected that and never kicked up a fuss. Peter is a thinking person so, if he had made that decision, I knew that he would have thought about it. I was able to understand how he felt; I can remember as a young person no longer wanting to go to church. In general it is not a cool thing these days.

Because we were an army family we made it a priority to see our extended family often. I am sure that many people suffer as a result of constant moving, but the world is also full of suffering people who never moved home at all.

Tell me he is an addict. Tell me he is shocking. Tell me you are disgusted with all you think you know about him but *please* don't tell me that he was hauled around as an army child and suffered as a result. *It is simply not true.*

People often remark how visually alike Peter and I are. I can't see it myself (I have no tattoos) but I am able to see how much he resembles his father. They have many common traits: the same humour, their physical size, their love of the written word, their love of wearing hats. Actually, hats are a family trait – AmyJo has an amazing collection and I have an even larger one. My set of berets consists of twelve or more different colours. Years ago, when the children were little, they despised my berets (and we have our own jokes about them now). More recently, they've been encouraging me to wear them.

Peter and his dad have a love of vinyl records – an art form in itself. All of the children, bar Emily, have record players and love to play vinyl. My husband has about six or seven thousand records in his collection. He used to collect records here and there for Peter, too: the Smiths, the Clash, punk and Indie bands from the seventies and eighties, and many, many others. It was always his intention to leave this collection to Peter.

As a family we were very close, all of us. We were also a busy family: no lying in at our house in the morning. Most weekends, whilst we were living in Germany, Peter's dad would take the two older children on IVVs – a German national pastime – which stands for International Volk Vanderungs. These were ten-to-twenty-kilometre walks all over the country. An IVV would often involve driving for an hour or more just to take part, and then they would walk or run, see a lot of the countryside, chat and, at the end, hopefully bring home a trophy or medal. We still have a huge box full of all these trophies.

When Emily got older, she and I would take part as well. We always played games together and involved the whole family in each child's particular pursuit, whatever it was. We did so many things together.

There was discipline, but it was tempered with love. I wouldn't allow any of the children to hang around on street corners. Peter told me recently that I was stricter than his dad had been – which shocked me, but I can believe him. It's his perception and I can't argue with that. Often army dads have to go away for periods of time and mums have to adapt to the change. You have to be two-parents-in-one at times.

When their dad was away, once, for several months, it was a worrying time for the children – they missed him terribly – but we managed the best we could, knowing that he was doing his duty. The weeks go by quickly enough, but it can be harder at weekends; so we would ensure that, each Saturday night, the children and I would dress up and visit a different restaurant. We took it in turn to choose a place and the rule was that we couldn't pick the same place two weeks on the trot. It was actually good fun. Emily was three and she only ever chose McDonald's or the Chinese – not that she actually ate in the Chinese, she just loved to play with their beaded curtain each time she visited the toilet (and she made a point of visiting the toilet often). I was lucky when it was a McDonald's trip as it usually cost me very little. We would organise Tramps' Lunches for all the children in our neighbourhood, awarding a prize for the best-dressed tramp — a contradiction in terms. We'd put up posters to advertise the event and serve sausage and chips in newspaper.

All the children were very close indeed. I have video footage that they took themselves which covers so many years. They would make up plays together and interview each other. Peter and AmyJo have always had a special bond — they were so close in age — and nothing will change that. Peter's relationship with Emily was different. He was always the big brother and I laugh when I remember how worried he had been as an eight-year-old when Emily was just a few weeks old. 'Mummy, how can we ever teach her to speak?' he asked. These days we can't shut her up.

Both sisters find it particularly hard not to have time alone with Peter: to have to track him down only to share him with other people. It is even harder for me to have to rely on others to get a message to him. It has been especially difficult in the past to have to call strangers to inquire about my own son, but it is a small price to pay to know where he is and that he is safe. I have little pride left in that respect and have learnt that pride can get in the way of a lot of things. If it's only pride that prevents me from asking someone, yet again, if they have seen Peter, then that's what has to go.

Emily has found the past three years particularly hard going. She's now part of an age group that is impressionable when it comes to people and events and the music scene. I remember a girl fan who was attempting to meet Peter. She had travelled quite a long way and I slipped out to meet her while he was asleep. She was the seventeen-year-old daughter of a doctor from Surrey and totally enamoured with my son. I told her that Peter was very sick and that she should be revising for her forthcoming exams. Emily was, then, also seventeen and it would be upsetting to think that she could be doing the same thing. I just treated this young lady as I would hope anyone would treat my daughter, and I tried to explain to her that she shouldn't lavish her attention on somebody who was ill.

We sat for an hour or so and I bought her coffee and a bite to eat and saw her back onto her train home. I would like to think that I had talked some sense into her. The point is that Emily has never been drawn to Peter's lifestyle, even though she could so easily have been. Poor Emily had little peace at school as her chums would always be texting her messages about what Peter had been up to, or sending texted questions – so much so that she left school in the middle of her A-levels to escape the fuss. Understandably, this upset her dad immensely; there have been far-reaching consequences as a result of Peter's Albion adventure.

Both Emily and AmyJo just want their brother to be well and that they be left in peace to get on with their lives. They are not interested in all the other idiosyncrasies that are involved with being a Doherty these days.

By the end of April 2006, Peter had been given – in addition to his already long list of offences and multiple arrests – a twelve-month community order and an eighteen-month drug-rehabilitation sentence (which were extended to two years). However, things did seem better – usually a sign of trouble ahead in the Peter Problem. For all the thousands and thousands of pounds spent on his various rehabs and implants, all of which may look like a waste of time – at best a preventative and delaying tactic, prolonging the inevitable of Peter reaching his rock bottom – it was to be a court order in the form of probation that would begin to bring about a change in Peter's attitude and a new and positive outlook. He now has to report regularly to the probation service. Locking someone up in prison does no good unless there is help in there to address patterns of behaviour; help in the form of people with the skills needed to assist an addict in reaching the point where he can face himself and deal with that without the use of chemicals to numb whatever it is he (or she) can't face.

Thanks to the courts, Peter is now somewhere along that process and trying harder than ever to overcome his problems. I hear very positive feedback from him. This is the key to his recovery. We usually believe that which we say ourselves. It doesn't matter what other people tell us or even what we know in our hearts or minds: unless we speak it ourselves, it can rarely help.

There is a theory regarding the cycle of change, used as an illustration for any pattern of behaviour. I first came across it many years ago in connection with a four-day course I attended called 'Helping Clients Change'. It was for health professionals to assist their clients in modifying their behaviour and could be included for everything from smoking cessation to drinking and sexual behaviour.

Imagine a circle and that wherever you are on that circle defines how you will proceed. For example, imagine that you smoke and want to give up. In order for you to be able to give up smoking, certain processes have to occur. Very often, people fail at their first attempt, *but this is normal.* None of Peter's failed rehabs or attempts to stop taking drugs were a waste of time. It has all been part of his cycle of change. Some people move around the circle more quickly, many people more slowly, and many never complete their cycle. Many die.

Family life continued, but not as we knew it. There are many untold tragic stories of how we have coped as a family. How my husband and I have coped and are coping; how the wider family are coping as they see our pain and witness the negative effects of living life as we now know it.

In the Doherty home there has been much sadness, marked at times with a severe, deafeningly silent anger that screams at you from every wall in every room. Mixed with the sadness and the anger is the constant pain, the sorrow, the feeling of foreboding, the embarrassment, the guilt, the shame, the unhappiness, the helplessness, and the utter hopelessness of our situation. For my part, I have tried so hard to sprinkle love over all this negativity; it is my profound belief that only love will see us through.

Each of us has a different experience of the Peter Problem because we all hold different roles in the dynamics of our family. Each of us feels our own individual pain is hard to bear and seeks to cope with that pain and all its effects in the only way we know how. If you were to ask me who I feel has suffered the most as a result, then I wouldn't hesitate to say my husband. Up until this point in time, I have been able to keep most of what has happened over the past three years – the really intimate changes in our family's situation – hidden, with only a few trusted friends and family knowing and looking on aghast as our world was falling apart.

As a couple, our children have always been very important to us. Each of our three children was wanted and loved. There is no 'second child' syndrome in our family: we not only wanted a second child but the icing on the cake was that we had a little boy.

Peter senior and I always endeavoured to put each child's welfare before our own and, although they weren't spoiled with expensive toys, they were spoiled by the sheer amount of time we spent with them all throughout their growing years and, in particular, in their adolescence.

Of course, I am sure we failed many times as parents and only the children can comment on this; but, hand on heart, I can say that we truly took our responsibilities seriously. We tried to nurture without stifling, love without spoiling, to be there for all of them and to uphold a united front. We encouraged each of them and hoped – as most parents do – that, when they were ready to take their place in society, they would be happy and healthy and live a fruitful life as decent, law-abiding citizens, giving to life rather than taking, and having a strong sense of what was right and what was wrong.

When there were difficult moments – such as when the kids saw their peers behaving in a particular way, knowing that they wouldn't be allowed to follow suit. Then, we had a family phrase that their dad coined, and which each of the children knew well: 'There are many advantages to being in this family, however, there are a few disadvantages . . .' Meaning that there were times when the answer was just 'No', so accept it.

Trying to be 'wise as serpents and gentle as doves', we ensured that the children were kept busy and close to us. As a family, we enjoyed activities together and made sure that there was room for the individual to develop within that framework.

None of the children were ever 'bored' (or boring) because they always had so much to do. There was rarely any bickering.. AmyJo and Peter were together for eight years before Emily was born and they had (and still have) a unique bond and always played very well together. If occasions arose where there were disagreements, then their dad would remind them that we were a family and that it was better for them to agree to disagree than to argue. He said that the world was full of squabbling people and we didn't need it at home. It upset me earlier this month when someone said it had been reported in the press that AmyJo had now abandoned Peter. I rang him to assure him that this wasn't true.

'I never take any notice of what they write about me and nor should you,' he said, but that is easier said than done.

When Emily was born, the dynamics changed. Both AmyJo and Peter were enamoured with her and so protective of her, but it would be Peter who would tease Emily, as brothers do. However, they were still very close. When AmyJo returned home from University during the holidays, she and Peter usually had planned some surprise that invariably involved dressing up, a song, and a sketch or two.

Peter and his dad had so much in common. They shared a love of an endless list of such TV comedies as 'Only Fools and Horses', 'Blackadder', 'Fawlty Towers', and 'Hancock'. They could quote whole passages of a sketch and would be in a world of their own. They were both members of the Tony Hancock Appreciation Society – they still have the neckties to prove it – and one year they went to a Hancock Convention.

They both loved Chas & Dave and the early black-and-white Ealing Studio films. They played chess and squash and, in his teenage years, Peter would accompany us most Monday evenings to an auction in Rugby where he'd usually buy old books by the boxful. They also, of course, shared a passion for football and, when Peter embarked on his QPR fanzine, it was his dad who encouraged him most.

As with any family, we have had our ups and downs. I don't want to give the impression that we were the epitome of happiness all the time. All families have issues to deal with and these are the very experiences that enable and empower individuals to cope with whatever comes along – they are character-building exercises.

The Peter Problem, though, is, at times, simply too large to handle. It is seemingly endless. If someone was able to say, 'By 2007 this will all be over; just hang on in there,' then I could see some hope at the end of the tunnel. If someone could say, 'Do this, and all the problems will be solved,' then it would all be tolerable.

Once we had returned to England, the pressure that we were under as a family began to take its toll on each of us, and I saw it as my responsibility to cater to everyone's needs with love, patience, understanding and encouragement as best I could. I tried to maintain the equilibrium under a very shaky set of circumstances, trying to keep a sense of humour – and praying all the while.

For my husband, the situation had become intolerable and Peter was no longer allowed home. We live in a goldfish bowl in the army and, whether true or not, the publicity that surrounded Peter was alarming and my husband needed to distance himself – emotionally, mentally, physically, professionally – from the whole thing. In one way, he adopted an approach that is often used with alcoholics and addicts and their families — an approach called 'tough love' which sends a message that says, 'This is no longer acceptable.'

We all approach problems in different ways and I respect my husband's views because that is the only way that he can deal with the situation. Likewise, he has allowed me to continue in the only way I know, and he respects my views even though he doesn't agree with them. There have been times when I've been asked by my husband not to mention Peter's name in front of him. This doesn't mean that he is hard; it means that he is hurting; that he is trying to blot it out; that he is coping in the only way he can.

My daughters have just had to roll with the problems, and I am so very proud of their attitude and so very grateful that, although they adore their brother, they haven't been seduced by his lifestyle or the pursuit of fame at any price. One daughter is regularly door-stepped by members of the press, but has never made a comment about her brother. Both girls have suffered immeasurably, both have witnessed the pain of their parents, and both are missing their brother terribly. I have often wondered, 'What if there had been another brother — would he have been able to keep Peter safe?' It's a silly thought because history has shown that a brother can't always help a brother. But I often clutch at anything, playing out different scenarios, re-writing history.

The members of our wider family have been a great source of strength for us. They have visited when appropriate and stayed away when we needed time alone, looking on and waiting to see how it would all pan out.

For my part, I have found it easy to be honest with friends and family and thank them all for their support. I have been inundated with letters and cards over the years and each one has touched my heart immensely.

Of course, Peter has no real idea how much we are affected by his shenanigans; how his Albion adventure, his lifestyle has hurt the very people who have been closest to him. He is oblivious to our pain while we struggle diligently to understand his.

On the occasions when we meet, there is never the time nor the opportunity to discuss these important issues and, if I were to nag on and on, I know that he would cut the contact completely. It's vital that I maintain some sort of connection but I always tell him that, once he is recovered, I am going to 'batter' him, (this is a good old Liverpudlian expression). I can't batter him now as he is battered on many fronts already. It's such a sad situation and such a waste of time, energy and money – such a waste of his life.

Perhaps if I were stronger, I could push my way into Peter's apartment and keep some semblance of order; simply not allow the current state of play to continue. I do feel very ashamed to say that I don't feel strong enough to do this and that, if I did, he'd probably move on and leave me there. In reality, how many twenty-seven-year-olds could bear to live with their mothers? A part of me wishes that I could do this; that I could take care of him. I wish I had the strength to roll my sleeves up, get stuck in and physically fight for him. But I have heard from the parents of other addicts or alcoholics who have tried this tack and failed. It all comes back to the addict needing to help himself. Peter needs to fight for himself.

There is plenty of help and advice available, all over the country, for families and friends of addicts or alcoholics, which is an indication of just how profound the problem has become. One can only hazard a guess as to where this is all going to end. An interesting fact is that, in 1960, there were only ninety-four heroin addicts on the Home Office Index. Current statistics show there are 56,000 registered addicts in the UK alone. This is astronomical – and very probably not a full account. The true number is thought to be around four times as big. This must be costing the UK taxpayer millions of pounds and, in terms of human misery, it's costing far, far more. These are human beings who've been sucked into a lifestyle they are unable to control, and each one of these drug addicts is a mother's son or daughter.

A colleague at work with growing children is rightly fearful. She thinks all drug pushers should be dumped on an island somewhere and left to their own devices (she kindly adds that fresh water and supplies of food could be dropped off each day). It sounds great, but it just isn't the answer. We will need the answer soon, though.

The extent of drug trafficking and consumption in other countries is also truly horrifying. It is a global problem, now, and not one that is set to recede: it merely multiplies.

In the meantime, the foundations of family life are being destroyed, and yet the strength of a nation is set in the humble family.

There has been an attempt to claw back some of the basic family traditions of late, with airtime and money allocated to programmes showing parents the benefits of taking control of their children, of addressing many of the downsides of allowing children too much of a free rein.

My own family now is a splintered one. We, too, have fallen victim to the many complex issues that face families with an addict in their midst.

Chapter 11

Keeping the Faith

Pactum serva – Keep the faith

IF THERE'S ONE thing worse than a raving drug addict it's a raving Christian. I should know. I had never wanted to become a Christian. They were all odd people using God as an emotional crutch. Or so I thought. And I thought that writing about my faith would be a sure-fire way of being vilified by all and sundry. However, it's so much a part of who I am and how I feel and how I deal with the Peter Problem that it's quite impossible to keep this part back.

So, how does a Scouser who was baptised a Presbyterian, confirmed in a Methodist church, with a Jewish father and a gentile mother, married to a Catholic, make sense or sensibility of her faith? Most people would be confused. Most people will be confused just reading that statement. When talking with other parents about what sustains me personally in these dark days, my conversation always harps back to my faith.

Sunday Mornings

Not for me a Damascus Road experience. My childhood years were spent attending the local Methodist church, which I loved: there was always so much going on – shows, pantomimes, garden parties, Sunday-school trips and jumble sales. In fact, I have on my dresser, here at home, a large blue-and-white meat platter that I purchased for threepence from the 'white elephant' stall back when I was a little girl. I would have been about ten years old and remember being fairly upset because they didn't have any white elephants for sale.

On a Saturday night, mum tied my hair up tightly in rags. This was a real torment – not only did I suffer all through the night but, to add insult to injury, I suffered most of the following day in being horribly teased by the other children for my corkscrew ringlets.

I never realised until I was much older that neither of my parents ever came to church. In fact, to be honest, I was usually the only person in the whole family to attend (today, I'm still the only person in the family who attends church).

Back then, my two brothers and I would all leave the house together, clean and decked out in our best clothes: me with my ringlets, and my two poor brothers each with his own torture to bear – a quiff, set in place with the help of sugared water and a metal contraption called a waver.

We all set off together with a generous amount of change for the collection plate but, like clockwork, at the top of the road my brothers would abandon me. They would then get a bus to the Pier Head in Liverpool, making sure they were back in time for lunch. They had a wonderful time each week, but so did I. There, at Sunday school, I heard incredible stories, learned Bible verses parrot fashion and sang songs that I've remembered all my life.

It has been at the darkest points in my life – when the Peter Problem was at its worst – that these Bible verses, songs, and memories of long-forgotten stories have popped up and given me courage when I most needed it, and wisdom and direction when I have felt 'lost'. I have reaped the rewards over and over again, through the years, from my time at Sunday school.

Cast Your Bread Upon the Water . . .

My mother was the epitome of kindness and compassion, a meek and humble soul. Whilst I was growing up, she would ensure that her children followed her example of caring for all of our neighbours who needed it. After school, in the winter months, we would have to ensure that the old folk had all their 'messages' (shopping it's called nowadays) and that they had enough coal brought up from the cellar to see them through the night. On a Saturday, mum would suggest that I wash their front step for them, which I was very happy to do – it would usually bring a threepenny reward.

When I asked my mum, much later on, why she never

went to church, she said she had never felt comfortable there. She was a smoker (she felt condemnation) and she was married to a Jew (she encountered prejudice). In fact, she felt so uncomfortable that it was easier not to go at all. In her later years, she loved attending church with me. Old and frail, she would insist on kneeling to pray. This was something that brought tears to my eyes and prevented me from praying myself: to see someone who was in such pain yet who insisted on kneeling, even though she knew it would make no difference – to Who she was praying to – whether she was lying in bed or kneeling uncomfortably. However, I felt quite unable to stop her because this was what she wanted to do. She liked coming to church on the many different army bases and often remarked how loving the atmosphere was.

Our Liverpool home was always open to anyone in trouble; there would always be a welcome for a stranger. Indeed, my own mum would never pass a beggar in the street and, I'm ashamed to say, I used to find this very annoying, especially when she could no longer walk. When she was eighty-four, I'd be pushing her wheelchair, in a rush to complete whatever needed doing, when she would spot yet another person begging and would point so that I'd change direction. 'Mother, you only encourage them to beg,' I'd say.

To this, she'd have a few stock answers. In addition to 'But for the grace of God go I', there was: 'It's made round to go round', 'I'm only giving back what's been given to me' and 'Entertain strangers unawares – they may be Angels'. Her party piece was, 'Cast your bread upon the water and it will come back cake'. That was a strange one. But she was right. I spend a lot of time thinking about her words.

PROMISES AND BLESSINGS

When I was fifteen or sixteen, going to church lost its appeal (remember, this was the late sixties); none of my friends went and the boys *outside* the church seemed more exciting. My next encounter with anything remotely spiritual was when, three years later, I was joining the military to do my nursing training. The chap in uniform at the recruitment office in Liverpool said that I was to be sworn in – the old practice of 'taking the Queen's Shilling' (recruiting sergeants used to give a shilling to new recruits). I had to hold a Bible and I remember the solemnity of the occasion as I promised to serve God, Queen and Country. It was a promise that I have kept to this day.

I rarely attended church during the early seventies unless I was on duty and a patient requested communion or to attend the hospital chapel – then, if work permitted, the ward sister would allow to me accompany the patient. Always, on the wards, there would be visiting chaplains, priests and scripture readers. During 1976, I would often read the lesson on a Thursday in the hospital chapel in Aldershot. There were a few nurses who were Christians but I largely avoided them, except for a lovely senior staff nurse called Wendy – I liked her because she was so much fun. I remember one day when, after an arduous shift, I returned to the nurses' home and joined Wendy for a coffee. She had a heavy cold and said that she'd prayed about it. I was so cross with her because I had just left a ward of very ill people and she had the audacity to pray for her cold. I told her outright what I thought, but she told me she believed that God was interested in every area of our lives. I remained unconvinced but was staggered because she spoke as though she knew God personally, in a real way. She never spoke of her faith to me again that I can remember and shortly afterwards she left Aldershot. We are still in touch after thirty years.

One day, early in November 1976, I bumped into our padre in Aldershot town centre. He demanded to know where I had been that previous Thursday as I had missed reading the lesson. 'Oh, I'm sorry, padre, I got married on Thursday,' I told him. 'Married!' he echoed in his Welsh singsong tones: 'Where did you get married?' I told him that I had been married by special licence at the registry office and he was livid. Can you imagine it? I was twenty-three and I'd had to get permission from matron to marry – and now I was being cross-examined by the padre! At least he hadn't asked 'Why the rush?' as had a number of people. There was no reason for the haste to marry, other than the fact that I had fallen in love – no babies were born until AmyJo in 1978!

Back on duty that day, a call came through from matron

(she was a wonderful woman but you didn't cross her) and I took it, fearful of what she was going to say.

'Ma'am?' I said. She informed me that I would be getting married in the garrison church on the following Thursday.

'Married? But ma'am, I *am* married.'

'Yes,' she said, 'but this will be your blessing.'

I attempted to tell her that my husband was a Catholic and probably wouldn't want the fuss, but there was no arguing. Matron said she had spoken to my husband's commanding officer and that my husband *would* be there.

I feel that God was watching over me even then, ensuring that His seal covered my marriage vows even when I never really gave Him a second thought. When making my marital vows in church, I felt the same solemnity of my promise as I had when I joined up.

Always a New Lesson

In 1978, shortly before the birth of our first child, I was given an exemplary discharge from the army – in those days one couldn't serve and have children. Of course it's very different now. I thoroughly enjoyed my six years in the military. The army life is a good one and I often wonder at the fact that it is probably the only employer in the world that makes provision for the spiritual life of its personnel. You can usually be sure that, wherever in the world you serve, there will always be a padre, chaplain or priest at your disposal.

Not long after this, my husband came home with news of

an impending posting. 'We're off to Ouston, in December,' he told me. When he returned to work I phoned the family: 'We're off to Houston,' I told them. I later found out it was Ouston, Northumberland, not Houston, Texas. This Ouston was approximately twelve miles outside Newcastle. Peter was born in 1979 during this posting.

During our time there, I began to help out at the Sunday school and really enjoyed it. After Ouston, we were posted to Catterick Garrison in North Yorkshire and I never went to church. But, late one November day as I was driving past one of the Garrison churches, I spotted that there was a drama production on that night and thought that AmyJo and Peter would enjoy it. AmyJo would have been almost four years old and Peter was two and a half. I wrapped them up in their little duffle coats, hats and gloves and set off for some fun. The production was going well when, suddenly, there was a voice behind the lectern, announcing: 'This is the voice of God'.

Little Peter asked out loud: 'Where's God?'

As he asked me that innocent question, I searched my mind and spontaneously said: 'God is in our hearts.' I had no idea what I meant or why I had said it.

During our stay in Catterick, we took every opportunity to travel back to Liverpool to visit grandparents and I'd take the opportunity to work as a temporary 'bank' staff nurse at the local teaching hospital. The children would go to bed in the early evening and I would go off to work.

One particular night when I was on duty, I attended a

patient calling out continuously from the adjoining ward. When I opened her door, I was faced with a pitiful sight: almost every limb was in plaster and she was anxious and tearful. She said, 'I wan' a fag.' No please or thank you but plenty of piped oxygen. I went in search of the nurses on the ward but they were busy and so I asked if could sit with this patient a while as I had a few spare minutes.

Their response shook my whole being. My response to their response shook my whole being. As they began to pass judgement on this patient, in their smart uniforms and their know-all manner, a thought came into my head – where from or why, I don't know. As they spoke about this patient in less than endearing terms, I could see, in my mind, the scene where Jesus is kneeling in the sand while an adulteress is being judged. 'You who is without sin, cast the first stone,' he says.

Another time, I was on night duty in Liverpool and had taken the shift handover report from the day sister. She had spoken of a patient with an unusual surname that I thought I recognised. Sometime later, while I was attending to this lady, I discovered that she was the neighbour whose step I had washed many years before as a little girl. She was very poorly but I gently reminded her of our previous encounter:

'It's me, Jackie, I used to wash your step,' I said.

She opened one eye to inspect me. 'Mm,' she said. 'You never washed it properly.'

Liverpool wit. The ward was in stitches (pardon the pun)

and a patient confided that this was the first time she'd heard her speak.

I believe these instances and many more were all the prompting of the Holy Spirit. I didn't know it then, but things were beginning to change in my heart and head. Most Christians believe in the Trinity, a triune God – God the Father, God the Son, and God the Holy Spirit. It's common knowledge but, back then, I didn't have a clue what it meant or how it could relate to me.

GRACE AND GOOD NEWS

We were about to get posted again – this time to Germany – and, before we'd even arrived, I'd decided that I would start going to church. In 1982, we arrived in Germany on Peter's third birthday and, sure enough, when Sunday came around I took the children to the local church. My life would never be the same again. I sat at the back; the church was quite full and the sermon delivered such an impact to my already questioning heart and mind that I was a little fearful of what was happening to me. I wanted to cry and I wanted to get up and leave (but the children had gone through to Sunday school and so I couldn't leave).

Some years before, in Liverpool, when we'd had the children baptised, the vicar shared his own faith with us. He was neither ashamed nor embarrassed to say that he'd invited Jesus into his heart. He spoke freely about this 'Holy Spirit' and how He would never leave us. I remember him saying that Jesus loves us as we are, in our sin. He loves the sinner not the sin. That Liverpool church had been packed, standing room only. A real Scouse vicar, he had them laughing (and crying) in the aisles.

Now, the padre in this church in Germany was speaking about Jesus, I couldn't wait to leave. There's no way I'd be going back there. Or so I thought.

When the following Sunday came around, there we were again – the children and I – in church. I was now fascinated with the wonderful things that I was hearing, if not still a little confused.

This padre had been a teacher in Africa with his wife and four children before he felt 'called' to the church. I remember he'd been a rugby player, too. One Sunday after church, his wife invited me back to their home for Sunday lunch (my husband was in England following a knee operation). I thanked her for her kindness and explained that I had the lunch all in hand and that the roast was in the oven. She gently touched my arm and I went bright red, knowing that I had just lied to the vicar's wife – and so blatantly. She reissued her invitation and I accepted. En route to their house, I told the children that we were having lunch with the padre and his family and explained that we would have to say 'grace' before the meal. I gave a few examples so they would know what was expected.

We arrived and were made to feel so welcome. There were six children between us and, when we eventually sat to eat, my children were waiting for the grace. When someone began to eat, Peter said: 'We haven't said grace.'

When I got home, I tried to read my Bible – an old King James version – which had hardly ever been opened and was written in a language (though poetic and beautiful) that I could scarcely understand. The next time I saw the padre I challenged him.

'How can you honestly tell me that you read the Bible? It's so boring.'

He gave me a Good News Bible and said that I should pray before I read it, that I should ask God to open my eyes and heart and to enlist the Holy Spirit to help me understand. There we were, 'The Holy Spirit' again. What did he mean? Off I went with this brand new Bible. Today it's not so much falling apart as hanging together. This book has been read and re-read so many times. There is so much of it that I still don't understand, but boring it isn't.

Some time later, sitting comfortably in church and listening to another challenging sermon, I heard the words 'He who is not with me is against me', and suddenly I felt extremely uncomfortable. I had heard other passages like this one where Jesus had said, 'Whoever is not against you is for you.' Panic. I had to come off the fence. In that instant I felt the power of those words. People say that God's word is like a two-edged sword. I felt just that in this instance. It struck me that, yes, I was going to church, but that I really had no idea of who God or Jesus – not to mention the 'Holy Spirit' – was. People can twist the Bible to defend whatever they want. Probably the most out-of-context verse used is

'Money is the root of all evil'. It should read '[For] the love of money is the root of all evil.'

Of course I wasn't against Jesus, as the passage had suggested, I just didn't know who he was. I tried hard to live a good life, yet I knew that I was very much sitting on a fence. I was a hypocrite, I was critical, proud, a sinner. That day, in an army church in Krefeld, West Germany (as it was known then), on a barracks that had once been used as a German Light Reconnaissance Unit during the war years, I surrendered my heart to Jesus and asked Him to take control of my life. Today I am still a sinner, but I am a saved sinner.

Oh, heavens. What was I going to tell my husband? He didn't share my faith and I felt he wouldn't understand. Later that evening, when the time was right, I prayed silently for the courage to be truthful. This was going to be a real bombshell.

'There's something I need to tell you. I've become a Christian,' I said.

'You've always been a Christian,' he replied.

'No, I've always been a churchgoer,' I said.

Over the years, people have said that I'm religious. I know some of Peter's friends have said that of me, but when they have met me they have remarked on how different I am to what they had expected. I am a realist. Faithful yes. Religious no. Faith is from God; religions are man-made.

In the eighties, one of my children was admitted to hospital in Northern Ireland for an emergency heart operation and a nurse asked me my religion. 'Christian,' I answered. 'A Catholic Christian or a Protestant Christian?' she persisted. I suppose I was being a little naughty, even though I understood why she had to ask (if my child needed a man of the cloth, who would they call?), because I merely added that the Bible I read made no mention of Catholics or Protestants – and, for good measure, told her that my father was a Jew. She, in turn, was proud to announce that our surname was spelt the Catholic way.

I suppose a summary of my Faith would be: after loving God – or trying to love Him – with all my heart, my soul and my mind, I also try to love my neighbour as myself. I believe that, if only we could keep these two Commandments, there would be no more problems in the world. I often fail and just pick myself up and start again in the knowledge that there is always forgiveness from God, even when we sometimes find it hard to forgive ourselves. There is so much to the Christian faith.

LOVE IS ALL YOU NEED

'Love . . . Over Law'

Do you listen like I to the news
Are you shocked anymore at their tales?
Do you sit there unemotionally listening?
Do you care if the Law system fails?

Have you heard about crime in our cities?
Have you read there's no room in our jails?
What's happened? Will man never change?
Are we doomed to run right off the rails?

Looking back this is nothing that's new.
Poor old Moses had a job on his hands
God gave him the commandments for living
These laws now in all lands still stands

And still, man cannot stop sinning
By the laws — he will always fall short
On his own he is lost before starting
Please listen whilst I just share a thought!

When Jesus came and was questioned
About which was the greatest commandment
He answered with insight and wisdom
While some had (and still have) total misunderstanding.

He came not to abolish the Law,
But to make their meanings come true.
Jesus said this in Matthew's Gospel
Is this gobbledygook to you ?

To keep the commandments is a good thing
But Jesus gave us a staggering word
About which of them all was the GREATEST
I'll tell you in case you've not heard.

He said . . . the greatest of all was to love God.
With all our hearts, and our souls, and our mind
And secondly . . . now this one's much harder
And calls for love of a much deeper kind

And it's this one that causes us problems
LOVE YOUR NEIGHBOUR AS YOURSELF
Let's not try to kid one another
We'd rather leave this on the shelf

Yet if only we could keep these two 'greats'
We'd have no need of the rest
We'd have no need of jail cells
No putting the Law to the test.

It's so easy and yet very hard
For neighbours can be hard to love
The key is not to rely on your own strength
But on God's help from above.

And so the world goes on in a sadness
Not knowing this power from above
Believers must show and tell of the difference
Of this great power that is simply called love.
Jackie Doherty, 1983

Peter's grandmother (my mother) was always saying 'But for the grace of God go I'. She judged no one and would often repeat the following verse:

'A Walk Around Oneself'

When you're criticising others, and find faults here and
    there,
A flaw or two to speak of, or a weakness you can tear;
When you're blaming someone's meanness or accusing
    someone's self,
It's time that you went out to take a walk around *your* self.

There are many human failings in the average of us all.
Many grave shortcomings in the short ones and the tall:
But when we think of evils that men lay upon themselves,
It's time we all went out to take a walk around *our*selves.

We need so often, in this life, a balancing of scales.
To see how much in us wins and how much in us fails.
And before we judge another, we should lay him on a shelf,
The finest plan to follow is to take a walk around oneself.
Anonymous

I have just removed from my handbag something that I have
carried around with me since 1975. It offers sympathy to
people whose lives are broken, people who find it easier to
break the law rather than keep it, people who have never
been taught right from wrong.

'Tell Them'

How can you blame them, the children of strife – who
never were taught the true values of life.
Untutored in that which concerns heart and soul – loveless,
undisciplined, out of control?
Nobody told them of Love's Golden Rule. What did they
learn in the home and at school?
Were their young minds ever sown with the seed – of
Christ and His gospel, the code and the creed?
Poor little creatures! What chance do they stand – against
all the evils now rife in this land.
What have they done to our once splendid youth? Pity
them, help them and tell them God's truth.
Patience Strong

FORGIVENESS

As a parent, I initially blamed myself for the Peter Problem,
but it's easier to blame other people and, for a while, I did.
I blamed the people around him. If only they hadn't done
this, if only they hadn't done that. I'd been doing just that.
Back in 2003, I was blaming a man called Wolfman – a
friend of Peter's who was also a songwriter, poet and addict
– for playing a part in Peter's problems.

I don't know how or where they met, and I'm not sure
why I blamed him in particular, but a seed of hate was
growing. When I mentioned it to Peter, he said that I wasn't
to blame Wolfman, that he'd made his own decisions and

that 'Wolf' was cool. Whenever I drove to work, I would have to pass through a Dutch village called Wolfskuul and even seeing the name would upset me. Often I would drive twenty minutes out of my way just to avoid it.

I realised that I held a hatred for Wolfman and I knew that, in order to move on and not be held hostage by my own fear and anger, I had to lay that hatred aside. But how was I going to ask for his forgiveness? At the very least he would think that I was a lunatic! Secondly, how was I going to get in touch with him? I couldn't answer these questions but knew that I had to make contact. So I sat and wrote Wolfman the following letter:

11 October 2003

Dear Wolfman,
Greetings from an Autumnal Holland. I'm sorry, I don't know your name and can't hazard a guess as to what it might be . . . For me the name 'Wolfman' has conjured up a thousand worries this past year, knowing that Peter was ruining his life, his soul, in your company — and, indeed, as a mother, I've hated the sound of your name. I believe we were in the same venue one evening — my daughter Emily saw you — but I was both very glad and so very sorry that I didn't see you.

Since then your very name has brought much fear to my heart.

Peter is very fond of you indeed and I know that; I once

shared with him how I blamed you for his demise. He said that I mustn't do that as he made his own choices.

I would now like to ask your forgiveness for the hate I have felt toward you in my heart.

I am a Christian and Jesus says we must love our enemies. I had felt that you were an enemy – as I blamed you for Peter's hedonism. I see now that Peter is fully to blame and I now wish you well indeed.

I will be praying for you constantly that the power heroin has over you will leave you for ever.

I don't know if you believe in God, Wolfman but that doesn't matter. He knows you, inside and out, and He loves you deeply and longs to see you restored; to be yourself. From the very little I know about you, you have great talent and are a fine fellow but your use of chemicals has crippled you.

I implore you today to call upon the name of Jesus and you can be delivered / transformed. I know it. I've seen it so many times. This is my prayer for you, son, to come heart to heart with your creator and to truly live again.

May God bless you richly with wisdom and peace in your heart.

I have no idea how to get this letter to you, no idea where you are, but I believe you will receive it . . . somehow.

With love in Him and His precious name,

Jackie

I had no idea how to get the letter to him, but I knew who his manager had been at one time and I sent it to him in an open envelope, inside another envelope, asking if he could somehow ensure the letter was delivered. This sounds easy enough to do but, given the circumstances, chances of success were not high. I didn't expect to hear anything at all.

Almost three weeks later, early one morning (although I think that in their case it was very late one night – they hadn't been to bed), Peter phoned to say Wolfman wanted to speak to me; he had received the letter. He thanked me for the letter and we talked for a little while. Today we're good friends.

When we did meet, some time later in a courtroom, we discovered that we had something in common. We both were fans of Marvin Gaye, the famous soul singer who, tragically, had been an addict and, after many failed attempts at rehab, had been killed by his own father.

Prodigals Returned

At the beginning of this book, I mentioned another book that has greatly helped me – *Prodigals and Those Who Love Them*, by Ruth Bell Graham. As well as offering lots of anecdotes, verses and stories, Bell Graham elects to write about some of the thousands of people who have been challenged and changed.

The first of these is Aurelius Augustine (whose mother Monica prayed for him for twenty-seven years). Augustine lived from AD354 to AD430 and Bell Graham says he 'cast off his simple faith in Christ for current heresies and a life given over to immorality'. She describes his 'vulgar revels of wild youth' but he was eventually guided to Rome where he again began to study the Christian faith.

During the time when Aurelius Augustine lived, it was definitely not 'cool' to be a Christian. They were likely to be fed to the lions. But Augustine changed the course of history for the Christian and, because of him, Christianity became popular. More than that, his writings touched people's hearts. He changed from a wild and chaotic young man – an utter hedonist, caught up with the Manichaeans, a religious cult from Persia – to become, as a Bishop, a torch bearer for the light of the New Testament and, eventually, an established Saint.

The second prodigal is the Englishman John Newton, a fearsome and very cruel man. He had been born in 1725 and, apparently, at the age of six, was reading Virgil in Latin. His mother had a deep faith and had taught him catechisms and portions of scripture. His father was a sea captain. His mother died when he was only six years old and from then on life was very hard for him. He had a troubled childhood and later joined the Royal Navy, but he was a notoriously cruel man who was profiteering from the slave trade.

One night, during a particularly nasty storm whilst out at sea, the captain of his ship said that it was because of him that this night they would perish. Newton replied, in effect, 'If that be the case, then the Lord have mercy upon us.' No sooner had he said it than he, himself, questioned why, since he paid no attention to God.

After that experience, Newton began to change. He grew increasingly unhappy about being in the slave trade and left the sea, eventually entering the ministry.

Newton went on to write many hymns including the immortal 'Amazing Grace', still being sung today in churches and on the football terraces. In his later life, he befriended William Wilberforce (whose own story of conversion is amazing), who was, in due course, instrumental in the passing of the abolition of slavery in this country.

Ruth Bell Graham gives us an account of Newton's hedonistic youth. She said '. . . few have sunk lower in sin, which just shows that nobody's hopeless', and also relates, in his own words, how he saw himself as 'an infidel and a libertine, unrestrained by convention or morality . . . a free thinker who actively tempted others into his way of life.'

An infidel and a *libertine*. I couldn't believe what I had read. Remember that Peter was in The Libertines back then, in 2003. How eerie is that? Surely this was more than just a coincidence. In stories such as these I could see that people could change from being the vilest, cruellest and most hedonistic human beings, to become forces for good.

Another famous person to whom she refers is the great Russian writer Fyodor Dostoyevsky who, funnily enough, is a firm favourite author of Peter's. He was one of Russia's greatest writers and one of his best-known novels is *Crime and Punishment*. Peter later told me that, while I had been reading about Dostoyevsky's life, he had been reading (not for the first time) *Crime and Punishment* while in prison in 2003.

Dostoyevsky was sentenced to death in 1849 for his part in revolutionary activities but, at the last minute, was reprieved by the Czar who sentenced him to ten years hard labour in Siberia. On Christmas Eve, he commenced his journey to the penal colony there where he spent a little over four years. As he arrived in Siberia, he was handed a copy of the New Testament by two women who told him to search its pages carefully and, between the pages, he found twenty-five roubles. But, much more than money, he found within its pages 'riches' beyond compare. The words therein were to sustain him throughout his arduous times in Siberia. They continued to support him in the years after that, for his life on his return from the penal colony was far from easy. It is written that forty thousand people followed his coffin to the grave when he died.

In almost all of Dostoyevsky's literature are references to the Prodigal Son parable from the New Testament that he loved so well.

The Parable of the Prodigal son deals with three leading characters, the obvious Prodigal, the loving and forgiving Father and the less-talked-about brother who is resentful – his position is an interesting one. In our everyday lives, each of us moves between these characters: the wayward person in need of forgiveness, the big brother – resentful and withholding forgiveness, and then, as we mature, the person willing and wanting to forgive.

'Up All Night'

(Written on the eve of Peter's admission to yet another rehab)

Up all night:
Like a hamster, scurrying . . . hurrying
Stashing here, storing there
Dashing through his tiny lair
Hiding, concealing for later use
The chance to continue his desired abuse.

Busy, busy . . . all through the night
Chiselling pillows and feathering stores
Marking the territory for illicit scores.

My son, like a hamster, walking the wheel.
Dodging and diving to make his next deal.
The cute little rodent . . . is a rodent no less.
As he lives like a rat in a godless mess.

No mother can save him, 'tis vainly to hope.
No ability to change, no ability to cope.
Lost in a labyrinth . . . Lost to a lie
The Libertine's freedom . . . freedom to die.

I sit and I pray with hope flickering at best.
Wishing and willing to get through this test.

Abandoning life for the abandoning child
But the child is a man . . . wayward and wild.

Arrogant, stubborn, demanding and cruel
Living 'his' way with no standard of rule.
Where gone is the listener, the joker, the lad?
Replaced by the demons that leave us all sad.

Yet, hope springs eternal . . . Within my 'lumped' breast
And Yes! we'll fight on to o'ercome this test
We'll fight and we'll pray. We'll scheme and we'll plan.
We'll banish the demons and restore us the man.
Jackie Doherty, June 2004

Chapter 12

Nothing is Wasted

Absit injuria verbis – Let injury
by words be absent

FOR ALL THE heartache and misery that human beings can go through in their lives – and it is clear that some people seem to have more than their fair share of trouble – then there may be great comfort in the three powerful but understated little words: 'Nothing is wasted.' Everything that one experiences, good or bad, can be used in a positive way.

Mentally, if we were able to see our lives in the form of a clean white piece of paper before us and were to imagine that someone had asked us to put down on the paper some of the things in our past (or even things in the present) that we don't like or aren't happy about; things that we find hard to bear that have happened to us; things that we don't like that we have done to others; things we wish we had done;

things that we wish we hadn't done – we'd be tempted, I think, to write them on the other side of the clean white sheet. This would be for a number of reasons: it could be an attempt to ensure that they remain hidden – on the other side of the paper – or it could be so as not to ruin the nice new clean page now in front of us. It could also, without even being aware of it, be the very basic act of compart-mentalising our lives as a crude sort of 'Right, that was then, this is now'.

For some people, sadly, it is clearly very difficult to over-come many of the things that life has thrown at them. I would never minimize the enormity of what some people go through and believe that, in many instances, professional help should be sought in an attempt to enable that person to lead a near-normal life. Rather, I am talking about the less traumatic events in our lives; sometimes the very little things that keep coming up from the past to haunt us. Indeed, I have such a thing that comes back to haunt me time and time again – at least one thing that I can put on this nice clean piece of white paper. And I relay it here because, whilst I am ashamed of it, it is, I believe, a normal childhood thing that we can all relate to.

Here goes. When I was young, about eight or nine, we had in our class a fellow pupil called S, who wasn't very popular. The boys would make fun of her, she was poor, her hair was never combed and she certainly never wore a ribbon in it (that gives my age away). No one would ever lend her a pencil sharpener when she needed one; and, certainly, whenever we had to partner up for any activity, she would always be left on her own. Each morning as she passed by to take her seat in class, the boys would start saying loudly, 'Pooh, pooh, can you smell that?' And yes, it's true; she often did smell.

I am almost in tears already – this has haunted me throughout my life – but worse than *my* feelings is the knowledge that S is probably in an awful state somewhere. Everyday must have been hell for her. I can honestly say that I never did anything nasty to her but I can't honestly say that I ever did anything nice. I wasn't for her, and therefore I was against her. I never helped her. I was a popular kid and could easily have turned that situation around. So I was a bully by default, by my inaction.

I would write this episode on the back of my piece of paper because I am ashamed of it, very ashamed. I knew right from wrong. My mother had always taught me about walking a mile in someone else's shoes in order to imagine how they are feeling. Hadn't she made me cry as she sang about a crippled child that no one would play with – there's a line in that song that haunts me to this day: 'Mummy, when I go to heaven will the angels laugh and say, just because I am a cripple I can't join them as they play?'

Hadn't she shown me about injustice and prejudice? About this time, in the late fifties/early sixties, my parents had a nightclub and restaurant in Liverpool, and the chef was a black man. He had a family and very little money but he was a very honourable man and believed in God. When their baby daughter was born, mum held the Baptismal reception at our house, but some of our neighbours were very upset by this: it was racial hatred in post-war Liverpool. Mum tried so hard to teach us not to judge a person by the colour of their skin or by their circumstances, but to try to look into that person's heart.

I rarely visit Liverpool these days but, whenever I have been there, I scour the faces of the people as they pass me by, looking for S. I long to apologise; I long to say to her how sorry I am that, by simply doing nothing, I too added to her misery and torment.

I cannot change her experience and I could never lessen the pain that she endured but, over the years, I have used this experience for good. I have taken from it and learned that, indeed, it is not wasted. All my own children know the name of this person as I have tried to teach them the same values in life. My eldest daughter is a teacher and takes the time and trouble to help stop this type of behaviour among her own class of children. Peter, my son, always looks for, and into, a person's heart and has always despised injustice and unkindness. And my youngest, too, has learnt from my lessons.

Nothing is wasted. Back in Germany I worked for six years as a nurse in an English school on a military base with boys and girls aged from eleven to eighteen. My health-promotion displays always included, when appropriate, the topic of 'bullying' and, when the opportunity presented itself, I chatted with individual children and related my story. S may have moved on but she has never left me.

This one tiny example tells you much about who I am and how I think. But, at the same time, it actually has no bearing whatsoever on who I am because I wanted you to know about it. I showed it willingly. The awful events of my life are on the other side of my piece of paper and you can't see that – it's hidden from you and contains things I'm not proud of and don't actually want you to know about. The information on the other side of the paper shows me as weak; it reveals a weakness in my character and, if you knew about it, you could use it against me; so I prefer to keep it hidden, filed away on the other side in a compartment that can't be opened by anyone but me. I only look at it myself when some relevant trigger – a smell, a song, a memory – forces me to.

For some people there is so much in their experiences that they don't like and would prefer wasn't there. I portrayed a very convenient example – an example that most people would have experienced at some time, and something that would have you believe that I am a nice person. I showed you something that would tug at your heartstrings, and this is what we do instinctively in life.

At the beginning of my story – in the Author's Note – I write about the façade that each and every one of us presents to the outside world. We do it so naturally we don't even know we are doing it. The businessman, the teacher, the pop star, the mother – all of us present only what we want people to know.

Most of us are very bad at articulating our feelings. We put up with things until they get so bad that we explode. I've spoken to so many divorced people over the years and often they have revealed that, if only they had been able to talk about their problems, things wouldn't have got so bad; that they might even have been able to sort it out.

The example that I gave about myself is innocuous – but what if I had shared some of my sorrow, my pain, the mistakes I've made? You would think differently of me then. Think about something in your own life that is too painful to go on the front of the clean white page as it would spoil what people thought of you or what you thought of yourself. How could you possibly turn that around? Maybe the experience that you regret or are ashamed of can help other people.

Nothing is wasted.

It is well known that counsellors working with alcoholics or drug addicts are sometimes people who have known addiction in their own lives; that they have also experienced the suffering of being or knowing an addict or alcoholic and are using their negative experiences for the good of others. Of course, they probably wish that they had never drunk or taken drugs or that life had been different, but life is not like that. We can't change anything in our lives that has happened but we do have the wonderful opportunity to use our negative events as something positive.

I realise that some people are completely unable to forgive themselves, unable to forgive others, unable to move on or even acknowledge their pain – and there is a real sadness in this. I believe resolutely in forgiveness. However, that is not a carte blanche for bad behaviour. There has to be a point of some remorse, of being sorry for what you've done rather than being sorry for being caught. I also believe that, even when forgiveness is shown, there is still the issue of the consequences to be sorted. Bad actions bring bad consequences that have to be managed.

If there is someone or something that you cannot forgive, think how this is affecting you. You cannot move on; you can't even bear to think about it without getting angry or crying or feeling many diverse emotions. I have recently been badly hurt by a member of my own family (not someone who appears in this book) and even to think about it makes me very angry. Indeed, at the moment, I never want to see this person again. In fact, I have been so badly affected by it that I cannot talk about it – it's way down on the back of my clean white paper – and I just want to move on. But, of course, I can't move on. It's in my face and all sorts of triggers remind me of it.

There's a justified hatred in my heart, but what am I going to do with this hatred? Do I leave it and let it fester (as it obviously has done)? Do I approach this individual and have a huge argument and say exactly what I feel? Or do I deal with it in the way that I have been taught, in the only way that will eventually give me peace in my heart and my mind, even though at this moment I want revenge? I want to undo the hurt they alone have caused.

There is not a single thing that I can do in this horrid situation that will alter what has happened but I know that, for my part, I have control over what will happen because it all depends on my reaction. The consequences will then be different – and they will have to be managed by us both. For me, as a person who believes in God, I clearly know what I have to do. You may not believe in anything and yet still believe in forgiveness – if you do, that's great, and you have my respect. It just means that each of us has reached our understanding in a different way.

I have, therefore, forgiven this person. Now I'm just trying to forget. How on earth can I expect God to forgive me my mistakes when I'm not even able to forgive the mistakes of another?

And yes, I do forgive my son Peter. I forgive him for turning our lives upside down. We'll just have to manage the consequences as best we can. However, and goodness only knows it has taken me forever to get to this important point, my poor husband is finding it very hard to do the same. It may come, but his experience of life has been very different from mine.

Of course, quite rightly, he's hurting, he's angry, he feels he's been treated very badly and he feels let down. Peter senior believes things *could* have been so different; that things *should* have been so different; he feels the unfairness of the wider picture. Hadn't he striven to ensure that the children reached their full potential?

Of course he misses his son. Of course he wants him to be well. And of course he cannot – just cannot – deal with it all: the endlessness of the situation, the awfulness, the shame, the guilt, the longing to just make it all right and for it all to go away; to get back to some normality.

To be able to sleep, not to be wandering around the house in the early hours, not to be scanning the news reading all the reams of copy about the Peter Problem in the hope that he'll know what it is that people are referring to when he's at work – and mostly, I suspect, just to be able to understand why this is happening.

If my experiences and thoughts can help just one other person, then writing this book will have been worth it. In fact, even before its completion, it has already caused a huge change in my life. My husband and I have waded through thirty years of photographs. We've seen again our Peter growing up through these photographs. We've looked at the snapshots of his life, and it has been so wonderful. We've seen him playing cricket and football for so many different teams in as many different countries. We've watched him swimming, running, fishing, skiing, mountain walking, camel riding, skating, riding his bike, abseiling, enjoying a day at the races, playing at home, at Beaver Scouts, at ease, acting, acting the fool, with his Nanny London, alone, as a baby, as a toddler, as a child, as a young man, as he is, as he was, asleep and awake.

Reading his school reports and marvelling at his

academic achievements has also been a very rewarding time for a husband and wife to share and, during this time, we've talked about the pain and the problems openly. We've finally been able to discuss forgiveness. We've been able to explain and explore the fact that the Peter Problem is not about us, though we must have played our part. We've had that nice clean sheet of paper in front of us and we've actually been able to discuss what's on the back. Yes, this story has been of great help so far in the least likely of places – my own home.

As human beings, there is nothing so bad or so awful for which we can't be forgiven. There is no place so low from which we cannot be set free and transformed. For the believer, there is always hope. History throws up such tales to show us, time and time again, how people have turned from a certain lifestyle to become a 'new man'

I heard this joke many, many years ago:

A tramp shuffles past Speaker's Corner. A socialist spots him from his soapbox and, not wanting to miss his opportunity, declares: 'Brothers, see that man! Socialism will put a new suit on that man!' The Christian, from his soapbox, counters with: 'Friends, that's nothing, Jesus can put a new man in that suit!'

Each of us has the ability to change wrong things in our lives. There is always forgiveness and, once we acknowledge our faults, then comes the chance to move on.

Ah, yes, there's the rub isn't it? On the one hand, there's the offer of forgiveness – so easy, so flowing, so good, so within one's grasp – but, look, you can't accept it without accepting the faults and offering some attempt at remorse. This is the crux, I believe, of why many of us find it so hard to forgive or to find forgiveness. It can simply be easier just to carry on. Why bother with all that tedious stuff? Leave it, let it fester – but it will, as I have known to my cost, come back to haunt you. Pride is at the heart of not showing forgiveness and, in some cases, of not accepting forgiveness.

For some people, then, it is much easier just to try to switch off the hurting; to try to ignore it; to hope it will go away. It won't. My husband is very much a problem solver. He will always attempt to rectify a problem because he's a very practical individual and can usually see a way around most things; but, in this instance, he feels out of his depth. He has no control whatsoever and, not seeing an end anywhere in sight, his hopes for salvaging anything out of all the mess has diminished – if not evaporated. My husband can no longer bear the pain of what he sees his son involved in. It is, therefore, easier for him at this time to pretend that he doesn't care.

If he really didn't care, he would take no joy in his grandson; he would have washed his hands of the whole situation. That would have been a very easy thing to do – many people deny their grandchildren when there hasn't been a marriage involved in the process. Many even do so where there has been a breakdown in a marriage. They don't bother to keep up the contact in some instances. But here I am forced to admit that Peter senior has been even more encouraged than me by Astile. Every few days, big Peter will ask how he is, whether I've heard from Lisa, whether I've heard any news of what Astile is up to. He is often the one who says, 'Let's see if he can come down to Dorset,' and asks me to ring Lisa. For my part, I am usually so busy, so driven by trying to keep on top of everything, trying to ensure that my husband, my children and any outstanding Peter problems are addressed, that I let the days slip by easily before grandad is at it again: 'Any news of the nipper?'

It breaks my heart at times to hear him call Astile the pet names that he once used to use for Peter, such as 'squire', 'billy bilo' or 'his lordship'. It's spoken so easily and naturally that he may not even be aware of what he is saying. Here is a man very nearly at the end of his military life – a career that has spanned four decades – who has tried to live a good life. However, over the past few years, he has been confronted daily with the escapades of his son who is ostensibly regarded as Britain's most famous drug addict. A poly-addict.

No, I don't blame my husband's response. He's coping in the only way he knows how.

One particular problem for Peter senior is that it's in his nature to believe everything he reads in black and white – libellous or nonsense though much of it is. One article had reported that he was an SAS war hero and that he had dived for the army at great peril to himself, removing explosives attached to a tanker during the Gulf War in the nineties.

Utter rubbish. We did actually laugh at this and it did provide the family with a few moments respite from the 'bad' news, but it just goes to prove that we ought not to believe everything that is written.

In time, perhaps we will be able to see the much bigger picture. I can see an analogy in the story of a carpet maker busily weaving his thread in and out, in and out, working away on the underside of the carpet, when all of a sudden the weaver weaves in some un-coordinating colour that makes it look all wrong. It shouldn't look like that, what a mess, he thinks, but he carries on laboriously until the carpet is complete to find that, when he turns it over, a beautiful pattern has emerged from the weave. Amid the chaos of changing coloured threads, and all the hard work that this added to the already difficult task of creating a carpet, there was a reason for it after all. The carpet weaver can see it in the finished article.

Nothing is wasted.

My husband is not alone in his response: many parents, children, husbands and wives can't face the challenges of life that are thrown at them. Some feel so overawed by the enormity of given problems that they walk away, unable to bear it. In a unit for the long-term sick, as it was then called, where I once worked, we had a respite bed where patients could stay to give them and their families a chance to catch their breath. It provided a change of scenery and a chance for the parents to gather their strength again. Over the years, this room was used by many different families with very different problems and needs, but it soon became apparent that often – not always, but often – there would only be a mum who visited, or there would only be a mother at home to cope. In the cases that I knew of, there were many families where the husband eventually just couldn't cope with the rigours of having a long-term sick child in the family. I never once heard these strong women pass judgement on their absent partners or their husbands; they never complained about what life had thrown at them. They weren't all Christians or people of any faith, they just got on with it and, what's more, they had such joy in their lives.

It was always a pleasure when they visited the unit and I am grateful to them for teaching me so much about the human condition, about real life and about the things that truly matter – such as true grit!

One young resident on the unit had a horrendous condition and, incredible though it seems, had also been abandoned by both parents. Thankfully, the patient never knew of the abandonment. I have no blame for the parents involved. They had reached their rock bottom and they would have to live with their decision. This was the only way they could deal with their situation at that time and, who knows, if they were able to gain some strength from going down their chosen route, some trigger in their psyche may bring about a rethink of the whole situation.

Many partners walk out on their families. This is the only

way that they can deal with what has gone on in their own lives. Others hang on through thick and thin when, perhaps, they should really have left their partner years ago.

In our circumstances, we cannot escape all the worries of the Peter Problem as they pop up in our lives – made worse by the television, the radio and the press. Others who have no knowledge of the true situation openly discuss our problems. I receive letters telling me what we should be doing – I am encouraged, often, to kidnap Peter.

Of course we would like to 'kidnap' Peter. Some of my husband's fellow officers have, in the past, even offered their support in this daring deed. There is the urgent feeling that we should be doing something – or, rather, be seen to be doing something. I am doing something: I am praying, I am loving, I am hoping, I am awaiting the prodigal's return.

For some unknown reason, this has happened to my family. I would much rather that it hadn't happened, believe me, but it has. It is upon us and it envelops every area of our lives, now, so we must learn to live with it and try not to let it destroy us. It has already almost torn us apart, and I don't take anything for granted in that respect, but I remember another thing that my mother often said: 'God fits the shoulders for the burden'. How she used to annoy me with her sayings but, my goodness, they have their use now. It suddenly feels as though everything she ever told me was to help me through these hard times. Thank heavens I never knew what was in store for me back then.

*

When Peter last visited home, for Christmas in 2004, he left behind many items – books, electrical equipment, clothes, thousands of letters from fans, and several guitars including an old Gibson acoustic. Peter has tried several times to get this guitar back but his dad won't allow it to leave the house; he just won't budge. In fact, he did say once to someone who rang to try and retrieve it, that he would sell it back to Peter. Doesn't that sound awful?

I later learned that Peter senior was hanging on to it for the future. It doesn't take much to work out that our son may end up penniless. Living the way he does costs money. He likes to live well. There is also the strong possibility that, because of his drug use, he will end up very ill or mentally impaired and will need to be cared for. He may need rehab again. He may need a roof over his head, and the Gibson will go part of the way to paying for that. I never understood this at the time. I had thought that his father was being dastardly, but it turns out that he was just being practical. We are not out of the woods yet – there is no clearing in sight. So the Gibson stays.

It has been a source of deep concern for us as parents to learn of the amount of money that Peter wastes or gives away and, worse, presumably spends on drugs.

In November 2005, AmyJo and I had attempted to meet him for breakfast one day in his hotel on Brick Lane – another part of London that he loves. When we arrived he was being interviewed by French and then by German journalists, so she and I sat next door to the hotel for two hours at a kerbside café. As he came out of the hotel for a photo shoot, he spotted us and went berserk. Why were we sitting in the rain on a kerb? There was a warm hotel next door where there was food in ample supply. During a break, he joined us, briefly, and we had a snatched ten minutes together before he had to do another interview. The first thing Peter said to me was that he had to get clean, and there was desperation in his voice.

'Arizona will be expensive,' he said. Not knowing what to answer, I asked him to tot up, quickly, the price of rehab and the price of his drugs. It was like a light going on in his head. He looked almost relieved. And while we were both thinking in money terms, I was also making a reference to one of his favourite writers – the quick-witted Oscar Wilde who had once quipped: 'A cynic is a person who knows the price of everything and the value of nothing.' The price of rehab is nothing if it works. Its value is quite immeasurable.

Nothing is wasted.

Chapter 13

Waking to a Nightmare

Id imperfectum manet dum confectum erit –
It ain't over until it's over

'Waking again to a nightmare'

Awoken again . . . to a nightmare
A never-ending torture
That grips your heart and mind and soul
And . . . aches . . . and aches . . . And aches

Awoken again . . . in a nightmare
That presses each aching thought
Crippling senses, disabling actions
Not reacting as one ought

Awoken again . . . no peace now
In dreams or when awake

A feeling of desolation
That your very heart will break.

There is no pill to 'fix it'
No cure to ease the pain
Awoken again . . . to the nightmare
Again . . . and . . . again . . . and again

My Son, My Son, why hast thou forsaken yourself?
Jackie Doherty, June 2004

For a drug addict or an alcoholic, there becomes a blurring of day and night, particularly, I suppose, in the music industry where it's normal to be up for most of the night during most of the week. For the loved one of an addict or an alcoholic, it is a double whammy. You lie there, night after night, unable to sleep because you're thinking of your loved one, or waiting for the phone to ring, or worrying about them, or praying long into the night for them. And each day can be very hard. You still have to get on with the normal routine of your day no matter how tired you are.

I do believe that, in the event of sleep deprivation, the body will eventually just take control and sleep will come. Once sleep has arrived, you (the addict's mother, husband, whoever you are) become oblivious to the events of the day that has passed. And you have no thoughts about the events to come. Until . . . that moment of waking when, quickly, without warning, it all starts flooding back. It wasn't a dream after all. It is a nightmare – a living nightmare – that no amount of sleep can take away because each and every day you have to wake up to it.

Ah, sleep! The mystery of life itself. A time of rest and recuperation. All living creatures need time to rest and humans are no exception. Oftentimes, in physical ill health and especially in mental ill health, sleep is an important but overlooked factor on the road to recovery; the buzz word among patients leaving hospital is, 'I'll be glad to get home for some sleep' – usually because wards can be very busy places.

Sleep is so important to everyone. But it's a joke with children, isn't it? As parents, we put them to bed when they don't want to sleep and wake them up when they do.

The mobile phone is such a wonderful invention – and yes, there is an off button – but I have to organise my mobile phone so that it will wake me up and, at the same time, not disturb my husband. It is usually in the wee small hours that I get various phone calls – and it's usually then that Peter rings me. The trouble that I have taken to ensure that I can answer calls with the minimum of fuss: I've worn a glove and put the phone inside; I've secured the phone under my pillow; I've even, dare I admit it, used various parts of my sleep attire to hold it in place. I consider myself very lucky that I don't need a lot of sleep. This has been a blessing in the Peter Problem.

However, it is the constant burden that being in this situation brings that has the most devastating effect in almost every area of my life. The worst thing is the awful, nagging desire to be able to get to sleep and never to wake up. That isn't a thought of suicide, it's an honest acknowledgement of how I often feel – partly because I have no control over the Peter Problem and partly because I often feel like I'm drowning.

I have spoken to so many other mothers in similar situations and it seems this is a common feeling among people who have a prodigal somewhere. The constant expectancy of a phone call, day or night, weighs heavy on a parent's heart. Whether you're awaiting good news or bad news, they both play a part in wearing down an individual. But always, running alongside these expectancies, is the unfailing hope, desire, yearning to hear from your child and to hell with the time of the call. It's always better to have a call at a strange hour than to not have a call at all. It makes a mother happy to get a phone call; there needn't be any conflict in the conversation – it's just important to let her know you are alive and okay.

'Sick and tired of being sick and tired.' For the uninitiated, this is a phrase that is bandied about among addicts, recovering addicts and addicts on the point of recovery.

As an addict's mother, this phrase could also so easily apply to me and to other mothers, parents, brothers, sisters, children and wives of addicts, in relation to how we feel, too. It is the most wearing position to be in – to know, hour by hour, that someone you love is addicted to something, something that is causing them harm, that could kill them and, above all, is preventing them from living a normal life.

The word addict comes from the Latin word *addictus* which means 'given over' – when someone was awarded to another as a slave. Today the meaning is no less pleasant: 'to become physiologically dependent, especially on a drug', or 'to devote oneself excessively or compulsively to something'. This, as we all know, can refer to any sort of addiction, be it gambling, smoking, sex, alcohol . . . the list is long.

Many people have addictive behaviours on a different level, such as obsessive-compulsive behaviour. With this, for example, they may be continually checking if they have switched the cooker off, knowing that they have but still having to check again. Sometimes, such behaviour is triggered by bad news or bereavement. This kind of dependency can be exhausting and, in some cases, can cause personal distress; but some people manage these compulsions fairly well and are able to contain them causing a minimum of disruption to their lives and the lives of others.

By contrast, at the other end of the scale, for the alcoholic or the drug addict, nothing, not their partner, their children, their parents, their job, not even self-esteem is important. Just the drink or the drug.

The addict would do anything for the next fix and this is the most sickening thought to have to bear. Crime – prostitution, theft, violence – committed in order to fund a habit, an all-consuming habit; likewise the drinker for another drink.

Meanwhile the ones closest to that person are in turmoil, waiting for it all to stop, doing what little they can to manage the situation. There will be no end until the addict becomes sick and tired of being sick and tired. It doesn't matter that those closest are sick and tired of being sick and tired. They don't have control. Even the addict doesn't have control. Control is held by the drug, or the alcohol, or the next bet. The addict has, in effect, handed over all control and, until he wakes up one day and thinks 'I don't want to do this anymore,' then change will never happen.

Some people say, in disgust, 'It's easy, just don't do it!' but these people don't understand addiction.

There are people – the proportions are epidemic – who are acutely and dangerously overweight in the United Kingdom. They are addicted to eating. They know that they shouldn't eat and that it isn't good for them; they know it makes them feel awful, but they just can't stop. They have given over their control.

As much as I believe that overweight people don't like being overweight or don't enjoy their habit, I believe the alcoholic or the drug addict shares the same emotions of self dislike, or to use a stronger term, self hate: they have the desire to stop, but are not be able to manage the triggers that cause them to abuse their bodies.

It isn't for any of us to condemn. The addict knows, deep

down, the pain they are causing, but they cannot address the pain until they understand why or how they are causing it. It would be no good for me to try to explain to Peter the pain that he has caused to most of the family at the moment. He has no idea what each of us has had to endure and if, for one split second, he was able to see the pain, it would cause him such unbearable suffering that he, like other addicts, would 'fix' his pain, since he can't fix ours. The eater, the drinker, the smoker, the gambler, the drug addict, the sex addict and others are all 'fixing' their emotions, doing or taking something that alters their mood. And so the cycle continues.

The addicts can and do 'fix' their problems, alter their moods, get rid of their pain, while the onlookers, the loved ones, are alone and floundering. Take heed, if you are an onlooker or a loved one of an addict, there is help out there for you, too. Don't try to go it alone because there are support groups all over the country for every sort of addiction. If you are sick and tired of being sick and tired yourself, then make it a priority to get some help. You cannot be expected to know how to cope in an alien situation.

This has been my loss, I am afraid to say; although I know that there are support groups out there for mums like me, I haven't felt that this was an avenue that I was able to explore very easily. The main reason is the overriding fear of the press finding out. Before now, I have endeavoured to keep a low profile, fearful of ridicule or embarrassment. I have been extremely lucky to be able to draw strength from my faith. I too, like the addict, am sick and tired of being sick and tired and just want it all to go away or stop. But that isn't going to happen. Yet.

It's a cliché – an overused or trite expression often used by people like me when telling their story – that the whole process has been cathartic. I didn't want to use this cliché, but I have to say that, if you are the loved one of an addict, do write things down because it does help to remember the facts. It helps to chart the course of the problem. It's a stark reminder of where it all started, as well as a frightening window through which to see where it may all go. But it also helps you remember the good times, and why you love your child so much.

My simple story, without the added dimension of the media interest, serves to remind me that not one of us can know what tomorrow may bring. It is not presented as an 'objet trouvé'. It is more the outpourings of a mother's troubled heart that have been cobbled together in the hope that the loved ones of addicts may take some solace in the fact that their situation is understood; and that they may try to make sense of their senseless situation – or seek help.

To answer the frequently asked question, 'What are your hopes for the future?' is both so very hard and fairly simple. The obvious answer – hope for a 'happy ending' where everything turns out well in the end – is far too simplistic and slips easily from the tongue but it's hardly realistic. The harder answer comes from a knowledge of the whole situation and the wider picture involved and has to be pulled from the recesses of the mind and dug from the beating chambers of the heart. Life is complex and an easy answer – given in some vain hope that it will satisfy the person that asked the question – will never suffice.

My hopes for the future are every bit as complex as the Peter Problem. Of course I want him 'well'. Naturally I'd like the family reunited in every way – indeed my heart aches for life as it used to be. But these are vain hopes.

I am a realist and know that my life will never be the same again. Nevertheless, I also believe that there could be even better times ahead for all of us; that the best is yet to come. Wow! What a hope for the future. Each of us must learn to make the very best of what life throws at us and not allow circumstances to break our spirit. I believe that the human spirit can actually be strengthened by adversity – and history is full of stories that support this. Wherever there is human suffering there is evidence of human endurance.

This endurance, perseverance, hope – call it what you will – comes from many sources. It can even come from negative feelings, such as those that drive a person to revenge. Sheer stubbornness or obduracy has helped many to withstand great challenges or trials. For me, as a very weak person, it is only my faith that keeps me strong. Sadly, this is not the answer for everyone, nor would I be so insensitive as to suggest that it is.

So, the more difficult answer to the question 'What do I hope for?' has to encompass all the relevant details of the Peter Problem. Peter Doherty is an intelligent, thinking person and is very much aware of his imperfections (would that we all were). It is not enough to give a list of wishes or desires other than those already mentioned. No, the answer would have to get to the root of the problem. Therein lies the real answer — at the root.

On the face of it Peter's life is chaotic and disorderly and, in that respect, just like the lives of a lot of people. However, he is in the limelight and so we see his life, in detail, everyday. Chaos for me goes against the grain — I'm the type of person who needs order and orderliness. Peter's creativity and his ideas and his reasoning may well be stifled by orderliness. Many artists and thinkers seem to be afflicted by such a dichotomy.

It is, therefore, hard to hope for 'order' in Peter's life as it might just crush his soul.

He will tell you that he believes in love so I must, as his mother, surely hope that love will see him through. Maybe this love will enable my son to live his life in a way that brings meaning for him.

My hopes for his future would be very different to his hopes for the future, but I know that no amount of wishing, nagging and haranguing will benefit him in any way. I have used them all to no great effect.

I have tried very hard to understand his line of thinking. It isn't enough to read biographies or books about other people with addictions, and it isn't enough for me to talk to other addicts or to educate myself on addiction issues as they may bear little resemblance to Peter's own story. There may be alarming similarities between some of them, but I know that no two stories are exactly the same.

Peter is enigmatic and he does have charisma. The Peter I once knew had enormous passion for the things he believed in. I think these qualities still exist and I have been a witness to them. One time when he was in rehab and wasn't feeling very well, he pulled out a letter from a fan that warranted a reply and asked me if I would write and thank them for their well wishes. He couldn't rest until I had finished and had shown him the written letter ready to post.

Peter's fans have meant a great deal to him over the years and I have ended up writing to many. I recall going with his younger sister and some other members of the family to see him at the first gig he played in Frome, Somerset, at the Cheese and Grain. I had no idea where the venue was and stopped the car to ask a well-dressed man the way.

'Are you going to see Pete Doherty?' he asked me.

'No,' I replied. 'I'm going to see Babyshambles.' I had been taken aback that he knew the band, never mind knew an individual in the band.

I was surprised to learn that this well-dressed man was also on his way to see the gig because he looked so respectable! Later on in the evening, I chatted to him and learned that he had followed Peter around the country. He said he would never miss an opportunity to see him – something so many fans have told me. It didn't really matter if Peter failed to turn up because he knew that Peter wouldn't let his fans down if he could possibly avoid it – i.e., it would take something out of his control to prevent him from appearing. Others have been very frank with me and said they couldn't risk missing one of his gigs in case that turned out to be his very last performance. I tried not to let the tears flow when I was told that but, as much as it broke my heart, I understood it. In his crazy days, many went to the gigs for exactly that reason – to see my son die.

His fans take many forms: youngsters, teenagers, men and women. One evening last year, I went to see Babyshambles in Bristol with Emily and some of our cousins. AmyJo came up from London and joined us later. It was such a wonderful gig. We spent time with Peter before and after the show and, just before we left, AmyJo insisted I met one of Peter's fans who had travelled from Wales. They had waited so long to see him – and now wanted to meet me. I don't usually want to get involved with meeting fans and so I was reluctant but I didn't want to appear rude. I was stunned to meet a lady older than me. She was such a genuine person. She said that Peter had really helped her son who had been through a rough patch, that she travelled to all of Peter's gigs and that she loved him so much. It was surreal.

These positive stories rarely appear in the press, but I hear them often from people who know Peter.

My ultimate hope about the future – not taking into account what Peter thinks is probably best for him – is for him to abstain completely from any chemicals. This hope would include there being peace, love and understanding between father and son and all parties involved, and my finding the sense in all of this mess so that others may be helped by my story and may find hope themselves and even empathy from me for their own story.

My prayers are slightly different. They are short. Unceasing but short. I just ask for strength for the day ahead.

I must end as I began . . . knowing that there is no end. Knowing that there will be more tears to come, more bumpy ground to tread.

Mine is a mother's tale. If you were looking for sleaze and shocking stories, then this has not been the book for you and I am sorry if it has left you feeling cheated. But I am hoping that you may just have been able, through my simple story, to understand a little of what goes on behind the headlines that you read.

Further than this, perhaps there will be a few of you who will have been able to take up the unwritten challenges found here from page to page – to examine your own hearts and to open your eyes fully to what is happening in our society. You will not have found any answers unless your own heart was ready to hear the truth.

Peter may never become a penitent prodigal. He may never turn from his present lifestyle and may never have true peace in his heart. He may never know the forgiveness of God but, whilst I have breath in my body, I shall continue to pray for him, whether he wants me to or not.

Until then, he'll remain:

Peter the drug addict
Peter the prisoner
Peter the errant father
Peter the poet
Peter the prolific writer
Peter the singer
Peter my prodigal son.

Postscript

IT'S LATE JUNE 2006 and Peter is in France, I think, at a gig with his band.

All my hopes have been poured out and spread across these pages for all to see.

I have spoken about my Faith.

I have spoken about my Hope.

I have spoken about my Love.

'Meanwhile these three remain: faith, hope and charity' (Corinthians, 13:13).

It is now time to concentrate all my hopes on what's to come. It's always darkest before the dawn – and there's no point even mentioning who used to say that.

Afterword

A Note From Peter Doherty Senior

FROM MY PERSPECTIVE, it's difficult to know where it all went wrong. The natural inclination is to lay the blame elsewhere. It helps you cope – absolving your responsibilities and passing the buck. But ultimately you have to accept ownership. Ownership of the problem.

I have met a number of my son's colleagues and fellow travellers – all victims in one way or another.

When I was a kid growing up in London, it was rare for a policeman to knock on your door – wherever you went there were 'bobbies on the beat' so, if you committed a minor transgression, you'd be dealt with long before you made it back home.

Life was hard and you made your own luck. If you didn't work, you didn't eat. Pride and dignity were values instilled in you – standards that are sadly lacking today.

Life for me, growing up in London, centred on football in the winter and cricket in the summer. When I went into the army, everything about it appealed to me – the comradeship, the sport, the physical challenges and the mental toughness. Suddenly this kid, whose furthest excursion had been to go to watch QPR play at Coventry, was hauling himself out of monsoon ditches, standing near the top of Mount Kenya, shivering in the chill of an early African sunrise – or in the even chillier temperatures of a Belfast sunrise – awaiting whatever fate.

The military-family system is unique. Living in service housing in far-flung places has many drawbacks but also many advantages. Soldiers and their dependents are subject to military as well as local laws, which leads to a safe, disciplined environment. But this tends to make some family members feel claustrophobic and somewhat isolated from the rest of society. The military – and my corps in particular – is very much a family. And I have been a part of this family for over thirty years.

I am a Major in the Army, but this conjures up a stereotyped and jaundiced view. For most people, the Army officer is from a privileged background with a clipped British accept – like the Major in 'Fawlty Towers' or, indeed, the pompous Mainwaring from 'Dad's Army'. Nothing could be further from the truth.

As it is for most fathers, the arrival of a son was, for me, something to be heralded. I believe that whilst your kids are dependent on you, you have every right to set the ground rules and call the shots. Once they reach adulthood, it's a different kettle of fish. You become mates. It's not like 'The Waltons', but I have friends whose adult children ring up on a regular basis and who go to football matches together.

I was a strict disciplinarian at work and this was a trait I instilled in my children. Part of the kids' development, as far as I was concerned, was to teach them the value of money and to develop a strong work ethic. To that end, both Peter and AmyJo had paper rounds (free local papers) during two of our postings; we had a small camper van and it was very much a joint effort.

I was always involved in a sport and used to coach football. Peter loved playing football but eventually turned his attention more to his studies. His final few years of schooling were spent in Warwickshire. He was developing academically and, although he lost interest in playing football, he became ever more obsessed with following QPR. He decided to create his own fanzine called 'All Quiet on the Western Avenue'. Armed with an Amstrad computer, he wrote and edited it, printed it off and, with the help of his cousin Adam, flogged it at QPR home and away games. It was his pride and joy and everyone was impressed by his efforts.

I started to run car-boot sales on camp to raise money for both the unit and local charities. Peter and I would go to the local auction and buy shed-loads of books and, once he'd taken what he wanted, he would sell the remainder at the sale. He'd spend all his time reading and chatting with the punters. Peter was fascinated by a number of classic poets and writers, especially Oscar Wilde. I have no doubt that Wilde's self-destructiveness and penchant for mind-altering additions to his diet were prevalent in Peter's mind. Wilde had always harboured a desire to take opium; he had also developed a love for music.

In the summer of 1997, Peter moved up to London to stay with his gran as he'd been given a place at a London university.

I had watched with pride and excitement as his band, The Libertines, developed and received more airplay, write-ups in the *NME* and even mentions in the national press. He became a celebrity and, of course, in the small military community, his fame grew.

I remember that once he played at a small venue in Cologne, near where Jackie and I were living. It was a private affair, laid on for the benefit of the German rock 'n' roll media. We spent some time on the tour bus with drummer Gary Powell and bassist John Hassall whilst Peter and Carl Barât were giving interviews. When they came on stage, the energy they generated was incredible – they obviously had something. Afterwards we chatted for a bit, but Peter was distant, vacant. I thought he was pissed at the time.

After that, The Libertines went straight to America and I suppose it was downhill from there. From what I was reading on the various websites that had sprung up, things were going from bad to worse. Public fall-outs, cancelled tours and private gigs in his flat which would incur the wrath of not only his neighbours but the law.

I watched frustrated from afar as the public drama of his turbulent world heaved between drugs and brushes with the law; periods in Pentonville and rehab. His mother kept in contact with him. I dealt with it as only I could.

One time, he had gathered up all his belongings in an attempt to get well and came down to our house in Dorset with his personal possessions in an assortment of bags and boxes. We talked long into the night – lots of tears and promises and looking forward to new dawns. He was determined to put his life back on track. It never happened.

Peter's greatest misfortune was to become famous. I watched as he was voted one of the most influential rock heroes of all time in the *NME*. People seem hell-bent on perpetuating his wretchedness – a pathetic, limp figure.

And so I have to sit back and remember all those old, forgotten, far-off things – take some solace from some of the qualities that Peter has and the pleasure he gives to so many people. As parents, we seem to have given him a number of these qualities so it's frustrating that he has never had the strength to fight off this wretchedness.

I hope that one day he does.